# Spark Birds

POLYCHAETE

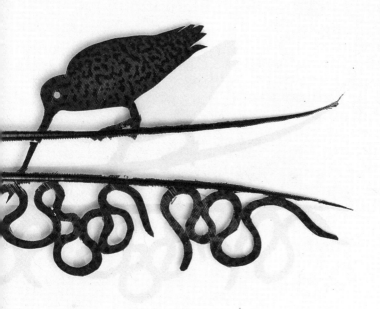

# Spark Birds

Essays and poems about owls, cranes, thrushes,
finches, penguins, petrels, and buzzards—
and the people who love them

FOREWORD BY
Jonathan Franzen

SHADOW BOXES BY
Chris Maynard

ORION
MAGAZINE

Published by *Orion* magazine.
All essays appeared in *Orion* except Jonathan Franzen's foreword.
© 2023 *Orion* magazine

*Orion* magazine
200 Main Street
Suite 2A, Northampton, MA 01060
orionmagazine.org

Editors: Jonathan Franzen, Christopher Cox
Editorial Production Manager: Tara Rae Miner
Editorial Interns: Ruby Rorty, Allyssa Foster
Cover and interior illustrations: Chris Maynard | featherfolio.com
Designer: Hans Teensma | impressinc.com

This book was made possible by a donation from the CDQ Charitable Trust.

COVER ART:
*A Star is Born* (front) and *Six Downward Birds*, detail (back) by Chris Maynard

ISBN: 978-0-913098-16-5

Printed in Canada. Inside pages are printed on 100% PCW recycled paper.

*Someday we'll live in the sky.*

—MARY OLIVER

# TABLE OF CONTENTS

CACTUS WREN STUDY

JONATHAN FRANZEN

# Foreword

THE BIBLE is a foundational text in Western literature, ignored at an aspiring writer's hazard, and when I was younger I had the ambition to read it cover to cover. After breezing through the early stories and slogging through the religious laws, which were at least of sociological interest, I chose to cut myself some slack with Kings and Chronicles, whose lists of patriarchs and their many sons seemed no more necessary to read every word of than a phone book. With judicious skimming, I made it to the end of Job. But then came the Psalms, and there my ambition foundered. Although a few of the Psalms are memorable (*The Lord is my shepherd*), in the main they're incredibly repetitive. Again and again the refrain: Life is challenging but God is good. To enjoy the Psalms, to appreciate the nuances of devotion they register, to connect with the emotions that engendered them, you had to be a believer. You had to love God, which I didn't. And so I set the book aside.

Only later, when I came to love birds, did I see that my problem with the Psalms hadn't simply been my lack of belief. A deeper problem was their genre. From the joy I experience, daily, in seeing the goldfinches in my birdbath, or in hearing an agitated wren behind my back fence, I can imagine the joy that a believer finds in God. Joy can be as strong as Everclear or as mild as Coors Light, but it's never not joy: a blossoming in the heart, a yes to the world, a yes to being alive in it. I get a taste of this joy whenever I so much as hear a brown towhee's simple call. And so I would expect to be a person on whom a psalm to birds, a written celebration of their glory, has the same kind of effect that a biblical psalm has on a believer. Both the psalm writer and I experience the same joy, after all, and other bird lovers report being delighted by ornithological lyricism; by books like J. A. Baker's

*The Peregrine.* Many people I respect have urged *The Peregrine* on me. But every time I try to read it, I get mired in Baker's survey of the landscape in which he studied peregrine falcons. Baker himself acknowledges the impediment—"Detailed descriptions of landscapes are tedious"—while offering page after page of tediously detailed description. The book later becomes more readable, as Baker extols the capabilities of peregrines and tries to understand what it's like to be one. Even then, though, the main effect of his observations is to make me impatient to be outdoors myself, seeing falcons.

Sometimes I consider it a failing, a mark of writerly egotism, that I'd so much rather take private joy in birds, and in nature generally, than read another person's book about them. But I'm also mindful, as a writer, that we live in a world where nature is receding from everyday life as fast as any glacier. There's an urgent need to interest nonbelievers in nature, to make believers of them, to push them toward caring about preserving what's left of the nonhuman world, and I can't help suspecting that nonbelievers share my allergy to hymns of devotion.

The easiest part of editing this anthology was choosing the bird-themed poems that have appeared in *Orion* magazine. An irony of poetry for me is that, although formally the most psalmlike of genres, it's the genre least likely to trigger my allergy. In poetry, the writer's subjectivity is central and all-coordinating. If a bird appears in a poem, it's because the bird *means* something to the poet. I don't feel obliged to delight in the bird myself, because, in a poem, the bird is always already a figure for something else— for a thought or a feeling in the poet. Jim Harrison, writing of birds in "New World," seems also to be speaking of himself: "It's autumn and their intentions are in their blood." In almost all the poems collected here, the interface between the natural and the human is literal and concrete, such as the birds glimpsed flapping "just above / the parking structure in the Bronx" in Ralph Black's "Egrets." Among the poetry candidates that my coeditor, Christopher Cox, sent me for consideration, there wasn't one that didn't move me.

I was more selective with the prose pieces, in part because space is limited, in part because I wanted to see a variety of bird families represented, and in part because I have strong opinions about how to write about nature. I was happy to find appreciations of birds that are favorites of mine—storm petrels, pelicans, emperor penguins—and even happier to find Sandra Steingraber's gem of a piece about a species, the house sparrow, that was decidedly not a favorite. A theme of decline and loss, the recession of the natural world, runs through many of the essays, but the persistence of birds, and thus the persistence of hope for the natural world, is an equally prominent theme. I found hope, too, in substantial essays by J. Drew Lanham and Emily Raboteau, who bring much needed attention to identity groups long marginalized by natural historians and conservationists. And then, for fun, we get to know a domesticated chicken, brought sparklingly to life by Deb Olin Unferth.

Common to all the essays is that, by focusing not only on birds but on human characters, they avoid the pitfall of preaching only to the converted. The power of the Bible, as a document of persuasion, derives from its stories and their characters. If I were an evangelist, going door to door, I would steer well clear of the Psalms. I would start with the facts as I saw them: God created the universe, we humans sin against His laws, and Jesus was dispatched to redeem us, with momentous consequences. Everyone, believer and nonbeliever alike, enjoys a good story. And so it seems to me that the first rule of evangelical nature writing should be: Tell one.

Most nature writing tells *some* kind of story. A writer ventures out to a lovely local wetland or to a pristine forest, experiences the beauty of it, perceives a difference in the way time passes, feels connected to a deeper history or a larger web of life, continues down the trail, sees an eagle, hears a loon: this is, technically, a narrative. If the writer then breaks a leg or is menaced by a grizzly bear with cubs, it may even turn into an interesting story. More typically, though, the narrative remains little more than a formality, a pretext for reflection and description. The descriptions are, to be sure, well intentioned. A writer who's moved to joy by nature, and who hopes to spread the joy to others, understandably wishes to convey the particulars of what incited it. Unfortunately, no matter how felicitous the descriptions may be, the writer is competing with other media that a reader could be turning to instead, audiovisual media that actually show you the eagle or let you hear the loon. Ever since the advent of color photography and sound recording, lengthy descriptions have become problematic in all genres of writing, and they're especially problematic for the evangelizing nature writer. To describe a scene of nature well, the writer is hard pressed to avoid terminology that's foreign to readers who haven't already witnessed a similar sort of scene. Being a birder, I know what a ruby-crowned kinglet sounds like; if you write that a kinglet is chattering in a willow tree, I can hear the sound clearly. The very words *ruby-crowned kinglet* are pregnant and exciting to me. I will avidly read an unadorned list of the species—*black-headed grosbeak, lazuli bunting, blue-gray gnatcatcher*—that a friend saw on her morning walk. To me, as a birder, the list is a narrative in itself. To the unconverted reader, though, the list might as well say: *Ira the son of Ikkesh of Tekoa, Abi-ezer of Anathoth, Mebunnai the Hushathite* . . .

If birds are the writer's focus, there do exist good stories about individual birds (the red-tailed hawks of Central Park) and individual species (the long march of African flamingos, the nonstop transpacific flight of bar-tailed godwits), and I can tell, from the news-story links that nonbirding friends are forever forwarding to me, that reports of astonishing avian foibles and feats can overcome the general public's indifference to birds, at least momentarily. Whether such stories make converts—and I'll say it here explicitly: my interest is in making converts—is less clear. The science of birds and their conservation should be interesting to anyone with a modicum of intellectual curiosity, but the world abounds with things to be curious about. The bird-science writer is painfully aware that he or she has only a few hundred words with which to hook a lay reader into investing attention in a particular field of research. One tempting approach to this challenge is to begin in medias res, by a campfire at some picturesque or desolate location, and introduce us to the Researcher. He will have a bushy beard and play the mandolin. Or she will have fallen in love with birds on her grandfather's farm in Kentucky. They will be tough and obsessive, sometimes funny, always admirable. The danger with this approach is that, unless the Researcher emerges as the true subject of the piece, we readers may feel bait-and-switched—invited to believe that we're reading a story about people, when in fact the story is about a bird. In which case, it's fair to ask why we bothered getting to know the Researcher in the first place.

The paradox of nature writing is that, to succeed as evangelism, it can't only be about nature. E. O. Wilson may have been correct in adducing biophilia—a predisposition to be attracted to nature—as a universal genetic trait in human beings. To judge from the state of the planet, however, it's a trait all too rarely expressed. What most often activates the trait is its display by people in whom it's already activated. In my experience, if you ask a group of birders what got them into birds, four out of five will mention a parent, a teacher, a close friend, someone they had an intense personal connection with. If everyone in the world had a connection like this, the planet might not be in the shape it is. But the faithful are few, the unpersuaded are many. To reach readers who are wholly wrapped up in their humanness, unawakened to the natural world, it's not enough for writers to simply display their biophilia. Before the trait can be activated in others, the writing also needs to replicate the intensity of a personal relationship.

One of the forms this intensity can take is rhetorical. Speaking for myself—admittedly, as someone inundated with more nature writing than I could ever read—I'm a lot more likely to read an essay that begins, "I hate nature" than one that begins, "I love nature." I would hope, of course, that the writer doesn't really hate nature, at least not entirely. But look at what the initial provocation accomplishes. Although it risks alienating the already persuaded, it opens the door to skeptical readers and establishes a connection with them. If the essay then reveals itself to be an argument *for* nature, the opening salvo also ensures that the writing will be dynamic: will move from a point A to a very different point B. Movement like this is pleasurable to a reader. Fierce attitudes are pleasurable, even in the absence of forward movement. Give me the blistering prose of Joy Williams in "The Killing Game," a jeremiad against hunters and their culture, or "The Case Against Babies," as ferocious an antibirth statement as you'll ever read, in her perfectly titled collection *Ill Nature*. Indifference, not active hostility, is the greatest threat to the natural world, and whether you consider Williams hilarious or unhinged, heroic or unfair, it's impossible to be indifferent to her essays. Or give me Edward Abbey's *Desert Solitaire*, an account of his years in the Utah desert, in which he fans a simmering Thoreauvian misanthropy into white-hot fire and applies it to American consumer capitalism. Here again, you may not agree with the writer. You may wrinkle your progressive nose at Abbey's assumptions about "wilderness," his unacknowledged white-male privilege. What can't be denied is the intensity of his attitude. It sharpens his descriptions of the desert landscape and gives them a forensic purpose, a cutting edge.

A good way to achieve a sense of purpose, strong movement from point A toward point B, is by having an argument to make. The very existence of a piece of writing leads us to expect some kind of argument from it, if only an implicit argument for its existence. And if the reader isn't also offered an explicit argument, the writer may have an argument assigned to the piece, by the reader, to fill the void. I confess to having had the curmudgeonly thought, while reading an account of someone's visit to an exotic place like Borneo, that the conclusion to be drawn from it is that the writer has superior sensitivity to nature or superior luck in getting to go to such a place. This was surely not the intended argument. But avoiding the implication of "Admire me" or "Envy me" requires more attention to one's tone of written voice than one might guess. Unlike the evangelist who rings doorbells and beatifically declares that he's been saved, the tonally challenged nature writer can't see the doors being shut in his face. But the doors are there, and unconverted readers are shutting them.

Often, by making an argument, you can sidestep the tonal problem. An essay collection that's dear to me, *Tropical Nature*, by Adrian Forsyth and Ken Miyata, begins by serving up a set of facts about tropical rainforests. The facts are seemingly neutral, but they add up to a proposition: the rainforest is more varied, less fertile, less consistently rainy, more insidiously hostile, than the drenched and teeming "jungle" of popular imagination. It's a very simple proposition. And yet, right away, there's a case to be made in the ensuing essays—further expectations to be upended, new astonishments to be revealed. Wedded to an argument, the scientific facts speak far more compellingly to the glory of tropical nature than lyrical impressionism, and meanwhile Forsyth and Miyata, as neutral bringers of fact, remain immune to the suspicion of seeking admiration. The premise of Jennifer Ackerman's bestselling *The Genius of Birds* is likewise simple and sturdy: that "birdbrained" ought to be a compliment, not an insult. Richard Prum's 2017 book, *The Evolution of Beauty*, reached a wide audience by advancing the argument that Darwin's theory of sexual selection, which mainstream evolutionary biologists ignored or denigrated for more than a century, can explain all sorts of nonadaptive traits and behaviors in animals. Prum's book has its flaws—the prose is gluey, and Darwin's theory was perhaps not quite as forgotten as Prum represents it to have been—but the flaws didn't matter to me. As far as I could tell, within the self-contained world of the text, Prum was single-handedly correcting a historical injustice. The theory of sexual selection was an eye-opener for me, and I learned a lot of cool things about a group of tropical birds, the manakins, that I otherwise might never have known. Such is the power of a compelling argument.

For the nature writer who isn't a polemicist or a scientist, a third avenue
to intensity is to tell a story in which the focus is on nature but the dramatic
stakes are emphatically human. An exemplary book in this regard is Kenn
Kaufman's *Kingbird Highway*. Kaufman grew up in suburban Kansas in the
1960s, became an obsessive birder (nicknamed Kingbird), and conceived the
ambition, after he finished high school, of breaking the record for the most
American bird species seen in a calendar year. The book quickly establishes
breaking the record as the story's dramatic goal, the protagonist's coordi-
nating desire. And then, immediately, we're presented with a difficulty:
the teenaged Kaufman has no money. To visit every corner of the country
at the right time of year, a birder chasing the record needs to cover huge
distances, and Kaufman decides that the only way he can do it is by hitchhik-
ing. So now, in addition to a distant goal and a serious obstacle, we have the
promise of a classic road adventure. As Kaufman makes his way around the
country, he's attentive to the birds, of course, but also to the national mood
of the early 1970s, the social dynamics of bird-watching, the loss and degradation of natural habitat, the oddball characters along the way. And then the
book takes a beautiful turn. As life on the road exacts its toll on the narrator,
he feels increasingly lost and lonely. Despite its superficial focus on birds,
the book reveals itself to have been, all along, a coming-of-age story. Because
the story has led us to care about the teenaged Kaufman, we stop wondering
if he'll break the record and start asking more universally relatable questions: What's going to happen to this young man? Is he going to find his way
home? What sets *Kingbird Highway* apart from many other "Big Year" narra-
tives is that it ultimately ceases to matter how many species Kaufman sees
in a year. Only the birds themselves matter. They come to feel like the home
that he's been yearning for, the home that will never leave him.

Even if we could know what it's like to be a bird—and, pace J. A. Baker,
I don't think we ever really will—a bird is a creature of instinct, driven by
desires that are the opposite of personal, incapable of ethical ambivalence
or regret. For a wild animal, the dramatic stakes consist of survival and
reproduction, full stop. This can make for fascinating science, but, absent
heavy-duty anthropomorphizing or projection, a wild animal simply
doesn't have the particularity of self, defined by its history and its wishes
for the future, on which good storytelling depends. With a wild animal
character, there is only ever a point A: the animal is what it is and was and

always will be. For there to be a point B, a destination for a dramatic journey, only a human character will suffice. Narrative nature writing, at its most effective, places a person (often the author, writing in first person) in some kind of unresolved relationship with the natural world, provides the character with unanswered questions or an unattained goal, however large or small, and then deploys universally shared emotions—hope, anger, longing, frustration, embarrassment, disappointment—to engage a reader in the journey. If the writing succeeds in heightening a reader's interest in the natural world, it does so indirectly. We can't *make* a reader care about nature. All we can do is tell strong stories of people who do care, and hope that the caring is contagious.

STOP AND DROP

Kathleen Jamie

# Storm Petrel

*A flight of imagination on the back of a bird*

W E FOUND IT on Rona the very day we'd arrived, and in keeping it, maybe I imagined I could bring home something of
the sky and spaciousness of that island, at least for a while.
It wasn't the dead bird we saw, lying on the turf, not at
first, but a tiny wink of metal. I said, "Look, what's that?" and Stuart replied,
"Storm petrel. They breed here. But ringed—that's a real find."

So here it is on my desk, in a polyethylene sample bag. An ex–storm
petrel, just a clump of desiccated feather and bone, with a tiny ring on its
hooked-up leg. When you report a ringed bird, it's called a "recovery," but
this one was beyond all hope of that.

My five-volume wartime *Handbook of British Birds* says that storm petrels
are "essentially pelagic," they "never occur inland except as storm-driven
waifs." That's the kind of language they inspire. There's a lovely poem by
Richard Murphy, called "Storm Petrel," that begins:

> *Gypsy of the sea,*
> *in winter wambling over scurvy whaleroads*
> *jooking in the wake of ships . . .*

At only six inches long, dark brown with a white rump, somewhat like a
house martin, you'd think them too small to jook anywhere at all, never
mind in storms, but they manage fine and come ashore only to breed, in
crannies between stones, on islands and cliffs at the ocean's edge.

So the bird is small and the ring on its leg even smaller. Back at the shelter we had to peer at it down the wrong end of binoculars to make out the number and that terse, famous address: "British Museum London S7."

THE RINGS on other birds, bigger birds, gulls and suchlike, often have space for the word *inform*. "Inform British Museum," they say, which makes it sound as though the bird in question had transgressed somehow, had jumped parole. The *inform* makes the bird-ringing project sound imperious and Edwardian, which it was—Edwardian, anyway, because bird ringing began in 1909. But the storm petrel's leg is so twig thin, there is no room for an *inform*.

A few days after we got home, I did contact the British Museum through its website. There is a form with boxes to fill in:

*Ring number:* 2333551.
*Type of bird (if known):* Storm petrel.
*Sex of bird (if known):* Unknown.
*Age of bird (if known):* Unknown.
*Was the bird dead or alive?* Dead. *Recently (one week)?* Long dead. Desiccated corpse.
*What had happened to the bird (hit by a car, oiled, etc.)?* Possibly preyed upon.
*Where found?* Scotland. Island of North Rona.
*Where, more precisely?* The north-pointing peninsula called Fianuis.
*When found?* Early July.

I pressed "submit," and the form went off on its own mysterious flight, leaving me with the questions not asked:

*Smell of bird?* Mysterious, musky, like an unguent.
*Where found, even more precisely?* Under an earthfast rock, on a patch of gravel, almost at the point where the vegetation expires altogether, and the waves pound ashore.
*What kind of day?* A lively, companionable summer's afternoon, with a sun bright enough to glint on a tiny metal bead and make us notice it, the only man-made object in all that place.

IT WAS the twentieth century before it was ascertained that birds do actually migrate; it seemed so improbable that swallows, for example, flew all the way to southern Africa. They obviously vanished in autumn and reappeared in late spring, but some folks thought they just hid, or hibernated in the bottoms of ponds. Gilbert White frets around the subject of migration; he hedges his bets. When he was writing this letter of 1769, all options were open:

> When I used to rise in a morning last autumn, and see the swallows and martins clustering on the chimnies and thatch of the neighbouring cottages, I could not help being touched with a secret delight, mixed with some degree of mortification: with delight, to observe with how much ardour and punctuality those poor little birds obeyed the strong impulse towards migration, or hiding, imprinted on their minds by their great Creator; and with some degree of mortification, when I reflected that, after all our pains and enquiries, we are yet not quite certain to what regions they do migrate; and are still farther embarrassed to find that some do not actually migrate at all.

*Hibernaculum* is his word for the winter quarters a swallow repairs to, but where was this hibernaculum? His other words are interesting too. *Embarrassed* and *mortification* almost suggest that the Enlightenment just then dawning, all that science and discovery, might have been driven not by the will to master and possess nature but out of chagrin. As human beings, our ignorance was beginning to shame us, because we didn't know the least things, like where swallows went in winter.

THE BRITISH MUSEUM passes the forms on to the British Trust for Ornithology (BTO), which organizes bird ringing in the UK. So in due course a computer printout arrived from the BTO. It informed me that the storm petrel had been ringed twenty-four years previously, not on Rona, where we'd found it, but 170 miles northeast of there, on the island of Yell.

Yell—I knew that place. It's one of the northernmost of the Shetland Islands. Only the summer before, I'd been there with my friend Tim; we'd seen killer whales off the cliffs at Noss, and made a road trip north via the chain of ferries, passing farms and small towns and the oil terminal at Sullom Voe. We'd traversed Yell, then taken another ferry to the farther island of Unst and made our way to see the gannetry at Muckle Flugga. That was all one place, stored in one corner in my mind, but Rona was wholly different. Different direction, different culture: uninhabited, remote, and Hebridean.

As soon as I read the letter, though, a connection shot between them. Suddenly they were linked by a flight path, straight as an arrow. I knew maps, but not as the storm petrel does.

Perhaps if you were some sort of purist, if you carried a torch for "the wild" and believed in a pristine natural world over and beyond us, you might consider it an intrusion to catch a bird and make it wear a ring or a tag. Perhaps you'd consider that their man-made burden violates them in a way. I admit there was something uncomfortable about the metal ring soldiering on while the bird's corpse withered, but when I got the chart out, traced the route, measured the distance, and understood that, yes, of course, on a southwest bearing, you could swoop along certain channels from the North Sea through to the Atlantic, it was because this one ringed bird had extended my imagination. The ring showed only that it was wedded to the sea, and, if anything, the scale of its journeying made it seem even wilder than before.

RINGING PROVED that swallows indeed flew south and did not stupefy in the bottom of ponds, and ringing too showed that storm petrels do the same. They migrate from Shetland or Rona, or their many other breeding places, typically down to the vast pelagic hibernaculum off Namibia and South Africa. A few come to grief; become small, washed-up bodies on a faraway shore, some bearing a return address. An address! Ludicrous thing for a storm petrel to carry. "The Ocean" would be their address, save for those weeks when they're obliged to creep between stones to breed.

So that's why I keep the bird's remains here in this room, my own hibernaculum—if only for a while. It's just a tuft of feathers in a polyethylene bag, a tiny skull, and that silvery ring above its shrunken, black, webbed foot. I keep it for the intimacy, and for the petrel smell: fusty, musky, suggestive of a distant island in summer. And I keep it out of sheer respect, because in life, this ounce of a bird made twenty-four return trips the length of the Atlantic. Twenty-four at least—which is not bad at all, for a waif, wambling.

JIM HARRISON

# New World

This moment says no to the next.
Now is quite enough for the gathering birds
in the tall willows above the irrigation ditch.
It's autumn and their intentions are in their blood.
Looking up at these chattering birds I become dizzy
but statistics say old men fall down a lot.
The earth is fairly soft here, so far from the world
of cement where people must live to make a living.
Despite the New Covenant you can't eat the field's lilies.
Today I think I see a new cold wind rushing through the air.
Of course I stare up too long because I love cedar waxwings,
their nasalate click and hiss, their cantankerous joy.
I fall and the dogs come running. Mary licks my face.
I tell them that this is a world where falling is best.

Kimiko Hahn

# Standoffish

Like the Butter Butt  I am not known  *for winter hardiness*
  and yet I am also  *one tough bird* and

*can digest wax*  (those sweet-wax lips or those tiny wax bottles
of awful sweet liquid  as opposed to the Butter Butt's bayberry).  Yes and
  like the Butter Butt  I have a *yellow rump*  and
    not only *do hybrids occur*  in my ranges

I am    in fact    a hybrid.
Unlike the Butter Butt  I'm not  *always good company*

    even  and you may know this  *at arm's length.*

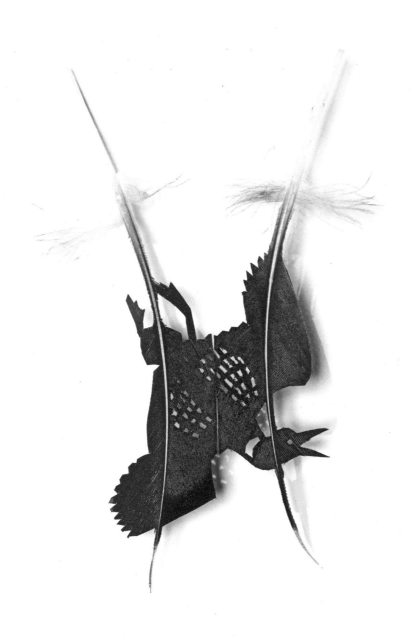

DIVING LOON STUDY

David Gessner

# Learning to Surf

*Because stability just might be overrated*

O
UT JUST BEYOND the breaking waves they sit there bobbing, two groups of animals, avian and human, pelicans and surfers. As they rise and fall on humps of water, the pelicans look entirely unperturbed, their foot-long bills pulled like blades into scabbards, fitting like puzzle pieces into the curves of their throats. The surfers, mostly kids, look equally casual. A girl lies supine on her board, looking up at the sky, one leg crossed over the other in an almost exaggerated posture of relaxation. For the most part the birds and surfers ignore each other, rising up and dropping down together as the whole ocean heaves and then sighs.

Pelicans are particularly buoyant birds, and they bob high on the water as the surfers paddle and shift in anticipation. There is no mistaking that this is the relatively tense calm of *before*, rest before exertion. Soon the waves pick up and the kids paddle furiously, gaining enough speed to pop up and ride the crests of breaking surf. They glide in toward the beach where I stand, the better ones carving the water and ducking under and cutting back up through the waves.

I just recently moved to this southern island town, but I have been here long enough to know that those who pursue this sport are guided by a kind of laid-back monomania. Each morning I bring my four-month-old daughter down to the local coffee shop, and each morning the talk is of one thing. The ocean, I've learned, is always referred to as *it*.

"What did it look like this morning?" one surfer asked another a few mornings back.

"Sloppy."

Remembering my own early morning glance at the water, I could understand what he meant, the way a series of waves came from the northwest, while another group muscled up from the south, and how the two collided and kicked up. Aesthetically it was beautiful, but practically, at least from a surfer's point of view, it made for a landscape of chop—not much to get excited about.

Another morning I heard this:

"How does it look today, dude?"

"Small."

"Nothing?"

"You can go out there if you want to build your morale."

It's easy enough to laugh at these kids, but I like the physical nature of their obsession, the way their lives center on being strong animals. In *When Elephants Weep*, Jeffrey Masson speculates that animals feel *funktionslust*, a German word meaning "pleasure taken in what one can do best." The strongest of the surfers, the ones who have grown up on the waves, must certainly feel this animal pleasure as they glide over and weave through the water.

I watch the surfers for a while longer, but when the pelicans lift off, I turn my focus toward their even more impressive athletic feats. Pelicans are huge and heavy birds, and the initial liftoff, as they turn into the wind and flap hard, is awkward. But once in the air they are all grace. They pull in their feet like landing gear and glide low between the troughs of the waves, then lift up to look for fish, flapping several times before coasting. If you watch them enough, a rhythm reveals itself: effort, *glide*, effort, *glide*. They are looking for small fish—menhaden or mullet most likely—and when they find what they are searching for, they gauge the depth of the fish, and therefore the necessary height of the dive, a gauging guided by both instinct and experience. Then they pause, lift, measure again, and finally, plunge. The birds bank and twist and plummet, following their divining-rod bills toward the water. A few of them even turn in the air in a way that gives the impression they are showing off. If they were awkward in takeoff, now they are glorious.

There is something symphonic about the way the group hits the water, one bird after another: *thwuck, thwuck, thwuck*. At the last second before contact, they become feathery arrows, thrusting their legs and wings backward and flattening their gular pouches. They are not tidy like terns and show no concern for the Olympian aesthetics of a small splash, hitting the surface with what looks like something close to recklessness. As soon as they strike the water, instinct triggers the opening of the huge pouch, and it umbrellas out, usually capturing fish, plural. While still underwater they turn again, often 180 degrees, so that when they emerge, they'll be facing into the wind for takeoff. And when they pop back up barely a second later, they almost instantly assume a sitting posture on the water, once again bobbing peacefully. It's a little like watching a man serve a tennis ball who then, after the follow-through, hops immediately into a La-Z-Boy.

THE PELICANS calm me, which is good. I have tried to maintain a relaxed attitude since moving to this island, but at times it's hard. I had vowed that I would stay forever on Cape Cod, my old home, but it was my writing about how much I loved the Cape that led to the offer of a teaching job in this overcrowded North Carolina resort town of outboard motors, condos, and southern accents. My wife, Nina, had just given birth to our daughter, Hadley, and the lure of health insurance and a steady paycheck was irresistible.

The truth is, the move has unsettled me: in coming to this new place, I find myself, and my confidence, getting shaky. If I've behaved well publicly, in the privacy of our new apartment I've at times started to fall apart. As each day unfolds, I grow ever less sure of myself.

One of the things that disorients me is the heat. It's the kind of heat that makes you want to lie down and give up, to start to cry and throw out your arms in surrender. I've known brutal cold in my life, but cold has the advantage of invigoration, at least initially. Now I understand the logic behind siestas; every instinct tells you to crawl to a cool, dank place and lie there and be still.

Lifting my daughter into our un-air-conditioned Honda Civic feels like sliding her into a kiln, so we are desperately trying to buy a new car. But today the Toyota guy calls with bad news. Our credit report has come back and our loan has been rejected.

"You have weak stability," he tells me, reading from the report.

I nod and consider the poetry of his words.

BUT THERE ARE other moments, moments when I sense that this may not be such a bad place to live. With summer ending, the parking lots have begun to empty. There are fewer beach walkers and more pelicans. Each

morning I take long walks with Hadley, and have begun to take field notes
on my daughter. I'm struck daily by her creatureliness, and the fact that this
squirming little apelike animal, barely two feet high, has somehow been
allowed to live in the same house with us. Nothing cuts through my doubts
about having moved here quite like this new ritual of walking with my daughter in a papooselike contraption on my chest. On good days we make it all the
way to the south end of the island where we stare out at the channel.

Many things have caught me off guard about being a father, but the most
startling thing has been the sheer animal pleasure. "Joy is the symptom by
which right conduct is measured," wrote Joseph Wood Krutch of Thoreau. If
that's true, then my conduct these days must be excellent.

This morning we watch two immature, first-year pelicans fly right over
the waves, belly to belly with their shadows. It's exhilarating the way they
lift up together and sink down again, roller-coastering, their wings nicking
the crests of the waves. Eight more adult birds skim right through the valley
between the waves, gliding by the surfers, sweeping upward before plopping
onto the water.

Feeling that it's only polite to get to know my new neighbors, I've begun
to read about the birds. I've learned that the reason they fly through the
troughs between the waves is to cut down on wind resistance, which means
they, like the surfers they fly past, are unintentional physicists. When I first
started watching pelicans, I kept waiting to hear their calls, expecting a kind
of loud *quack-quork,* like a cross between a raven and a duck. But my books
confirm what I have already noticed, that adult pelicans go through their
lives as near mutes. Whether perched atop a piling in classic silhouette or
crossing bills with a mate or bobbing in the surf, they remain silent.

Another group of adult birds heads out to the west, toward the channel,
as Hadley and I turn home. Before moving here, I never knew that pelicans
flew in formations. They are not quite as orderly as geese—their V's always
slightly out of whack—and the sight of them is strange and startling to
someone from the North. Each individual takes a turn at the head of the V,
because the lead bird exerts the most effort and energy while the birds that
follow draft the leader like bike racers. These platoons fly overhead at all
hours of day, appearing so obviously prehistoric that it seems odd to me that
people barely glance up, like ignoring a fleet of pterodactyls.

Yesterday I saw a bird point its great bill at the sky and then open its mouth until it seemed to almost invert its pouch. My reading informs me that these exercises are common, a way to stretch out the distensible gular pouch so that it maintains elasticity. Even more impressive, I learn that the pouch, when filled, can hold up to twenty-one pints—seventeen and a half pounds—of water.

"I have had a lifelong love affair with terns," wrote my friend from Cape Cod, John Hay, a writer whom I have always admired for his sense of rootedness. I've come to pelicans late and so can't have my own lifelong affair. But I am developing something of a crush.

I'M NOT a good watcher. Well, that's not exactly true. I'm a pretty good watcher. It's just that sooner or later I need to do more than watch. So today I am floating awkwardly on my neighbor Matt's surfboard, paddling with my legs in a frantic eggbeater motion, attempting this new sport in this new place while keeping one eye on the pelicans. Even though you can't bring your binoculars, it turns out that this is a great way to bird-watch. The pelicans fly close to my board, and for the first time I understand how enormous they are. I've read that they are fifty inches from bill to toe, and have six-and-a-half-foot wingspans, but these numbers don't convey the heft of their presence. One bird lands next to me and sits on the water, tucking its ancient bill into its throat. Up close its layered feathers look very unfeather-like, more like strips of petrified wood. I watch it bob effortlessly in the choppy ocean. Most birds with webbed feet have three toes, but brown pelicans have four, and their webbing is especially thick. Though this makes for awkward waddling on land, it also accounts for how comfortable the birds look in the water.

I'm not nearly as comfortable. Two days ago I spent an hour out here with Matt, and yesterday we came out again. Despite his patience and coaching, I never stood up on my board; in fact, I never made more than the most spastic attempts. Today has been no better. The best things about surfing so far are watching the birds and the way my body feels afterward when I am scalding myself in our outdoor shower. So it is with some surprise that I find myself staring back with anticipation as a series of good waves roll in, and it is with something close to shock that I find myself suddenly, mysteriously, riding on top of that one perfect (in my case, very small) wave. Before I have time to think, I realize that I am standing, actually standing up and surfing.

The next second I am thrown into the waves and smashed about.

But that is enough to get a taste for it.

I HAVE NOW been practicing my new art for three days. The pelicans have
been practicing theirs for thirty million years. It turns out that the reason
they look prehistoric is simple: they are. Fossils indicate that something
very close to the same bird we see today was among the very first birds to
take flight. They were performing their rituals—diving, feeding, courting,
mating, nesting—while the world froze and thawed, froze and thawed again,
and while man, adaptable and relatively frenetic, came down from the trees
and started messing with fire and farming and guns.

What struck me first about these curious-looking birds was the grace of
their flight. Not so the early ornithologists. In 1922, Arthur Cleveland Bent
wrote of their "grotesque and quiet dignity" and called them "silent, digni-
fied and stupid birds." A contemporary of Bent's, Stanley Clisby Arthur,
went even further, describing the pelicans' habits with something close to
ridicule. Arthur writes of the pelicans' "lugubrious expressions" and "pon-
derous, elephantine tread" and "undemonstrative habits," and says of their
mating rituals that "they are more befitting the solemnity of a funeral than
the joyous display attending most nuptials." His final insult is calling their
precious eggs "a lusterless white."

Even modern writers seem to feel the need to lay it on thick: as I read I
make a list of words that includes *gawky, awkward, comical, solemn, reserved,*
and, simply, *ugly.* It never occurred to me that pelicans were so preposter-
ous, though I'll admit that recently, as I kayaked by a sandbar full of birds,
I laughed while watching a pelican waddle through a crowd of terns, like
Gulliver among the Lilliputians. But "ugly" seems just mean-spirited.

When not seeing pelicans as comic or grotesque, human beings often
describe them as sedate and sagelike. Perhaps this springs from a dormant
human need to see in animals the qualities we wish we had. Compared to
our own harried, erratic lives, the lives of pelicans appear consistent, reliable,
even ritualistic, as befits a bird that has been doing what it's been doing for
thirty million years. And compared to their deep, consistent lives, my own
feels constantly reinvented, improvised. But before I get too down on myself,
I need to remember that's the kind of animal I am, built for change, for
adaptation. Long before we became dull practitioners of agriculture, human

beings were nomads, wanderers, capable of surviving in dozens of different environments.

Though barely able to hold their heads up at birth and fed regurgitated food by their parents while in the nest, newborn pelicans fledge within three months. The one-year-olds I watch flying overhead are already almost as capable as their parents, while my daughter will need our help and guidance for many years to come. But this too makes evolutionary sense: one reason for our long infancy and childhood is to give the human mind time to adapt creatively to thousands of different circumstances. Pelicans, on the other hand, are ruled by a few simple laws and behaviors. Still, at the risk of romanticizing, I like the sense of calm the birds exude, the sense of timelessness, of ritual and grace.

We humans face a different set of problems. Our bodies still run on rhythms we only half understand (and often ignore), and we have adapted ourselves beyond ritual. To a certain extent all rules are off. The life of a hunter or farmer, the life that all humans lived until recently, directly connected us to the worlds of animals and plants, and to the cycles of the seasons. Without these primal guidelines, we are left facing a kind of uncertainty that on good days offers a multifarious delight of options, and on bad days offers chaos. Ungrounded in this new place, I am acutely sensitive to both possibilities. And though it isn't comfortable building a foundation on uncertainty, it has the advantage of being consistent with reality. Maybe in this world the best we can do is to not make false claims for certainty, and try to ride as gracefully as we can on the uncertain.

THE HUMAN BRAIN is no match for depression, for the chaos of uprootedness. To try to turn our brains on ourselves, to think we can solve our own problems within ourselves, is to get lost in a hall of mirrors. But there is a world beyond the human world and that is a reason for hope. From a very selfish human perspective, we need more than the human.

Water and birds have always helped me live, have always lifted me beyond myself, and this morning I paddle out beyond the breakers and lie with my back to the surfboard just like the girl I saw in early fall. But though my legs may be crossed casually, I spend most of the time worrying about falling off. Even so, as I bob up and down on the waves, the whole ocean lifting and dropping below me, my niggling mind does quiet for a minute. And then it goes beyond quiet. I'm thinking of Hadley, sitting up now and holding her own bottle, and I feel my chest fill with the joy these small achievements bring. She will be a strong girl I suspect, an athlete. And, no doubt, if we stay here she will become a surfer, delighting in her own funktionslust.

Glancing up at the pelicans flying overhead, I notice that there is something slightly backward-leaning about their posture, particularly when they are searching for fish, as if they were peering over spectacles. From directly below they look like giant kingfishers. But when they pull in their wings, they change entirely: a prehistoric Bat-signal shining over Gotham. Then I see one bird with tattered feathers whose feet splay out crazily before he tucks to dive. When he tucks, dignity is regained, and the bird shoots into the water like a spear.

Inspired by that bird, I decide to turn my attention back to surfing. I catch a few waves, but catch them late, and so keep popping wheelies and being thrown off the surfboard. Then, after a while, I remember Matt telling me that I've been putting my weight too far back on the board. So on the next wave, almost without thinking, I shift my weight forward and pop right up. What surprises me most is how easy it is. I had allotted months for this advancement, but here I am, flying in toward the beach on top of a wave, its energy surging below. A wild giddiness fills me. It's cliché to say that I am completely in the present moment as this happens, and it's also not really true. Halfway to shore, I'm already imagining telling Nina about my great success, and near the end of my ride, as the great wave deposits me in knee-deep water, I find myself singing the *Hawaii Five-O* theme song right out loud.

Though no one is around I let out a little hoot, and by the time I jump off the board I'm laughing out loud. A week ago I watched some kids, who couldn't have been older than twelve or thirteen, as they ran down the beach on a Friday afternoon. Happy that school was out, they sprinted into the water before diving onto their boards and gliding into the froth of surf. I'm not sprinting, but I do turn around and walk the surfboard back out until I am hip deep, momentarily happy to be the animal I am, my whole self buzzing from a ride that has been more the result of grace than effort. Then, still laughing a little, I climb on top of the board and paddle back into the waves.

I COULD END on that note of grace, but it wouldn't be entirely accurate. The year doesn't conclude triumphantly with me astride the board, trumpets blaring, as I ride that great wave to shore. Instead, it moves forward in the quotidian way years do, extending deep into winter and then once again opening up into spring. As the days pass, my new place becomes less new, and the sight of the squadrons of pelicans loses some of its thrill. This too is perfectly natural, a process known in biology as habituation. Among both birds and humans, habituation is, according to my books, the "gradual reduction in the strength of a response due to repetitive stimulation." This is a fancy way of saying we get used to things.

While the pelican brain repeats ancient patterns, the human brain feeds on the new. On a biological level, novelty is vital to the human experience: at birth the human brain is wired so that it is attracted to the unfamiliar. I see this in my daughter as she begins to conduct more sophisticated experiments in the physical world. True, all of these experiments end the same way, with her putting the object of experimentation into her mouth, but soon enough she will move on to more sophisticated interactions with her environment. She's already beginning to attempt language and locomotion. Although pelicans her age are already diving for fish, she, as a *Homo sapiens*, can afford to spot *Pelecanus occidentalis* a lead. She will gain ground later. Her long primate infancy will allow her relatively enormous brain to develop in ways that are as foreign to the birds as their simplicity is to us, and will allow that brain to fly to places the birds can never reach.

Though I acknowledge these vast differences between bird and human, there is something fundamentally unifying in the two experiences of watching the pelicans and watching my daughter. There is a sense that both experiences help me fulfill Emerson's still vital dictum: "First, be a good animal." For me, fatherhood has intensified the possibility of loss, the sense that we live in a world of weak stability. But it has also given me a more direct connection to my animal self, and so, in the face of the world's chaos, I try to be a good animal. I get out on the water in an attempt to live closer to what the nature writer Henry Beston called "an elemental life."

I keep surfing into late fall, actually getting up a few times. But then one day I abruptly quit. On that day *it* is big, much too big for a beginner like me. I should understand this when I have trouble paddling out, the waves looming above me before throwing my board and self backward. And I should

HAWK SPIRAL

understand this as I wait to catch waves, the watery world lifting me higher than ever before. But despite the quiet voice that is telling me to go home I give it a try, and before I know it I am racing forward, triumphant and exhilarated, until the tip of my board dips under and the wave bullies into me from behind and I am thrown, rag-doll style, and held under by the wave. Then I'm tossed forward again, and the board, tethered to my foot by a safety strap, recoils and slams into my head. I do not black out; I emerge and stagger to the shore, touching my hand to the blood and sand on my face. The next night I teach my Forms of Creative Nonfiction class with a black eye.

So that is enough, you see. One of the new territories I am entering is that of middle age, and the world doesn't need too many middle-aged surfers.

I feared fatherhood, but most of the results of procreation have been delightful ones. One exception, however, is the way that disaster seems to loom around every corner—disaster that might befall my daughter, my wife, myself. No sense adding "death by surfing" to the list.

THOUGH I HAVE naturally begun to take the pelicans for granted, they still provide daily pleasures throughout the winter. What I lose in novelty, I gain in the early stages of intimacy. I see them everywhere: as I commute to work, they fly low in front of my windshield; they placidly perch atop the pilings while I sip my evening beer on the dock near our house; they bank above me as I drive over the drawbridge to town. My research reveals that in March they begin their annual ritual of mating: a male offers the female a twig for nest building and then, if she accepts, they bow to each other before embarking on the less elegant aspect of the ritual, the actual mating, which lasts no more than twenty seconds. These rituals are taking place, as they should, in privacy, twenty miles south on a tiny island in the mouth of the Cape Fear River. The eggs are laid in late March or early April and a month-long period of incubation begins.

Around the midpoint of incubation, my human family achieves its own milestone. Throughout the spring I have continued to carry my daughter down the beach to watch the pelicans fish, but today is different from the other days. Today, Hadley no longer rests in a pouch on my chest but walks beside me hand in hand.

I remind myself that the mushiness I feel at this moment, the sensation that some describe as sentimentality, also serves an evolutionary purpose.

With that softening comes a fierceness, a fierce need to protect and aid and sacrifice. This is not a theoretical thing but a biological one. In fact, this transformation borders the savage, and here too the pelicans have long served humans as myth and symbol. "I am like a pelican of the wilderness," reads Psalm 102. At some point, early Christians got it into their heads that pelicans fed their young with the blood from their own breasts, a mistake perhaps based on the red at the tip of some pelican bills, or less plausibly, on their habit of regurgitating their fishy meals for their young. Whatever the roots of this misapprehension, the birds became a symbol of both parental sacrifice and, on a grander scale, of Christ's own sacrifice. The images of pelicans as self-stabbing birds, turning on their own chests with their bills, were carved in stone and wood and still adorn churches all over Europe. Later, the parental symbol was sometimes reversed, so that Lear, railing against his famous ingrate offspring, calls them "those pelican daughters."

THE YEAR CULMINATES in a single day, a day full of green, each tree and bird defined sharply as if with silver edges. I kiss Nina and Hadley goodbye while they are still asleep and head out at dawn to the road where Walker will pick me up. Walker Golder is the deputy director of the North Carolina Audubon Society, a friend of a new friend, and today he takes me in a small outboard down to the islands at the mouth of the Cape Fear River. We bomb through a man-made canal called Snow's Cut and I smile stupidly at the clarity of the colors: the blue water, the brown eroding banks, the green above.

We stop at four islands. The southernmost of these is filled with ibis nests—11,504 to be exact. Ten percent of North America's ibises begin their lives here, and at one point we stand amid a snowy blizzard of birds, vivid white plumage and flaming bills swirling around us. Next we visit an island of terns, the whole colony seemingly in an irritable mood. This island, and its nearby twin, were formed when the river was dredged in the 1970s by the U.S. Army Corps of Engineers, which used the sand to consciously aid the Audubon Society in an attempt to create nesting grounds. Terns, like ibises and pelicans, require isolated breeding areas, preferably islands, and this human experiment, this marriage of birders and engineers, has worked to perfection. We watch as a pair of royal terns spiral above us in their courtship dance.

The terns are impressive, but the highlight of the day for me is North Pelican Island, the nesting ground of almost all of the pelicans I have watched over the last year. Hundreds of pelicans sit on their ground nests, some of which are as big as beanbag chairs. They watch impassively as we approach. The old naturalists might have called these birds "undemonstrative" and "lugubrious," but I'll go with "calm." In fact, while we're anthropomorphizing, I might as well put "Buddha-like" in front of calm. It's hard not to project this on them after experiencing the wild defensiveness of the tern colony. The pelicans barely glance up at us. Theirs is a much different survival strategy, a much quieter one, but natural for such a big bird with no native predators on these islands. I crunch up through the marsh elder and phragmites to a spot where two hundred or so pelicans are packed together, sitting on their nests, incubating. Some still have the rich chestnut patches on the backs of their heads and necks, a delightful chocolate brown: leftover breeding plumage. They sit in what I now recognize as their characteristic manner, swordlike bills tucked into the fronts of their long necks.

While the birds remain quiet and calm, there is a sense of urgency here. This marsh island, like most of the islands that pelicans breed on, is very close to sea level. One moon-tide storm could wash over it and drown out the season. It is a time of year marked by both wild hope and wild precariousness, danger and growth going hand in hand. The birds are never more vulnerable, and as a father, I know the feeling.

I'm not sure exactly what I gain from intertwining my own life with the lives of the animals I live near, but I enjoy it on a purely physical level. Maybe I hope that some of this calm, this sense of ritual, will be contagious. If the pelicans look lugubrious to some, their effect on me is anything but. And so I indulge myself for a moment and allow myself to feel unity with the ancient birds. It may sound trite to say that we are all brothers and sisters, all united, but it is also simply and biologically true. DNA undermines the myth of our species' uniqueness, and you don't need a science degree to reach this conclusion. We are animals, and when we pretend we are something better, we become something worse.

Having seen these fragile nesting grounds a thousand times before, Walker is to some extent habituated to them. He is also more responsible than any other human being for their protection. "We only visit briefly in the cool of the morning," he explains, "so not to disturb the birds." Playing tour guide, he walks in closer to the nests and gestures for me to follow. He points to some eggs that look anything but lusterless, and then to another nest where we see two birds, each just a day old. Though pelicans develop quickly, they are born featherless and blind, completely dependent on their parents, their lives a wild gamble. Heat regulation, Walker explains, is a big factor in nestling survival. Pelican parents must shade their young on hot days, and one dog let loose on this island while the owner gets out of his boat to take a leak could drive the parents from the nest, resulting in the deaths of hundreds of nestlings.

But we are not thinking about death, not right now. We are instead watching these tiny purple dinosaurs that could fit in the palm of your hand, the beginnings of their extravagant bills already in embryonic evidence. And then, in a neighboring nest an egg trembles. There's a tapping, and a pipping out from within.

A small blind purple head emerges from the shell. "Something only a mother could love," Walker says, and we laugh. But we are both in awe. It is the beginning of something, any idiot can see that. But what may be harder to see is that it is also a great and epic continuation.

While we watch, the almost pelican cracks through the eggshell, furious for life. Then it shakes off the bits of shell and steps out into a new and unknown world.

JEAN MONAHAN

# Afternoon with Brown Pelicans

A packet of brown and white
pelicans delivers itself
onto my wedge
of beach, sandbar
where a crowd of gulls
stands mesmerized by a stray cloud.

When I sidle close, the pelicans fasten
their clothespin faces
more tightly to the sand,
sage and suspicious.

One dips
a violin bow
over its shoulder
and commences to fiddle.

Another shrugs
its head
onto its back.

In a kind of yawn
one then another then another
distend their lower bills

in a gust-pouch,

      bubble-gum bubble
they struggle to control
as they stand and gargle
the wind.

      I did not know
what made air flow
supple and strange through
the world, what changed it from
cloud
to yawn,

every animal lung humming
vibrato of pelican,

wind's waterfall
slung into pelican pouches
across the beaches of the world
and wrung out as air:

light, new, breathable, pink.

As if nothing remarkable had happened,
the birds bring
the slide trombone of their bills
in close, lower pouch
deflated.

A dog barks, a surfer shouts.

The pelicans lift and I hold my breath.

Oh, everything, everything we have
is borrowed.

MARY OLIVER

# Owls

U PON THE DUNES and in the shaggy woodlands of the Provincelands, I have seen plenty of owls. Heard them at twilight and in
the dark, and near dawn. Watched them, flying over Great Pond,
flying over Rose Tasha's noisy barnyard, flying out of the open
fretwork of the spire of the old Methodist Church on Commercial Street,
where the pigeons sleep, and disappear one by one. I have seen them in
every part of the woods, favoring this or that acreage until the rabbits are
scarce and they move to new hunting grounds, and then, in a few seasons,
move back.

In January and February I walk in the woods and look for a large nest in
a tall tree. In my mind's eye I see the great horned, the early nester, sitting
upon her bulk of sticks, like an old woman on a raft.

I look in every part of the Provincelands that is within my walking range.
I look by Clapps Pond and Bennet Pond and Round Pond and Oak-Head
Pond. I look along the riding trail that borders the landfill—in the old days
a likely hunting ground and not one disdained by the owls or much else. I
look in the woods close to the airport, so often have I flushed an owl from
the pine trees there.

And I look in the woods around Pasture Pond, where, over a century ago,
Mr. George Washington Ready, once the Provincetown town crier, saw the
six-eyed sea serpent. He witnessed it, he said, emerging from the ocean and
slithering across the dunes. Into Pasture Pond it descended, and sank from
sight. Every winter I stare into the ice of the pond and think of it—still asleep,
I suppose, in the clasp of the lily roots, for no one has ever seen it again.

And I search in the deeper woods, past fire roads and the bike trail, among the black oaks and the taller pines, in the silent blue afternoons, when the sand is still frozen and the snow falls slowly and aimlessly, and the whole world smells like water in an iron cup. And I see, on my way to the owl's nest, many marvelous things—the gray hives of the paper wasps, hidden in summer by the leaves but now apparent on the boughs; nests, including one of the Baltimore oriole, with fish line woven into it, so that it has in the wind a comet's tail of rippling white threads; and pheasants, birds that were released into fall's russet fields but find themselves still alive at the far end of winter, and are glad of it, storming upward from the fields on their bright wings; and great blue herons thin and melancholy; and deer, in their gray winter coats, bounding through the cold bogs; an owl in a tree with an unexpected face—a barred owl, seen once and once only.

Finally the earth grows softer, and the buds on the trees swell, and the afternoon becomes a wider room to roam in, as the sun moves back from the south and the light grows stronger. The bluebirds come back, and the robins, and the song sparrows, and great robust flocks of blackbirds, and in the fields blackberry hoops put on a soft plum color, a restitution; the ice on the ponds begins to thunder, and between the slices is seen the strokes of its breaking up, a stutter of dark lightning. And then the winter is over, and again I have not found the great horned owl's nest.

But the owls themselves are not hard to find, silent and on the wing, with their ear tufts flat against their heads as they fly and their huge wings alternately gliding and flapping as they maneuver through the trees. Athena's owl of wisdom, and Merlin's companion, Archimedes, were screech owls surely, not this bird with the glassy gaze, restless on the bough, nothing but blood on its mind.

When the great horned is in the trees its razor-tipped toes rasp the limb, flakes of bark fall through the air and land on my shoulders while I look up at it, and listen to the heavy, crisp, breathy snapping of its hooked beak. The screech owl I can imagine on my wrist, also the delicate saw-whet that flies like a big soft moth down by Great Pond. And I can imagine sitting quietly before that luminous wanderer the snowy owl, and learning, from the white gleam of its feathers, something about the arctic. But the great horned I can't imagine in any such proximity—if one of those should touch me, it would be to the center of my life, and I must fall. They are the pure wild hunters of our world. They are swift and merciless upon the backs of rabbits, mice, voles, snakes, even skunks, even cats sitting in dusky yards, thinking peaceful thoughts. I have found the headless bodies of rabbits and blue jays, and known it was the great horned owl that did them in, taking the head only, for the owl has an insatiable craving for the taste of brains. I have walked with prudent caution down paths at twilight when the dogs were puppies. I know this bird. If it could, it would eat the whole world.

In the night, when the owl is less than exquisitely swift and perfect, the scream of the rabbit is terrible. But the scream of the owl, which is not of pain and hopelessness, and the fear of being plucked out of the world, but of the sheer rollicking glory of the death-bringer, is more terrible still. When I hear it resounding through the woods, and then the five black pellets of its song dropping like stones into the air, I know I am standing at the edge of the mystery, in which terror is naturally and abundantly part of life, part of even the most becalmed, intelligent, sunny life—as, for example, my own. The world where the owl is endlessly hungry and end-lessly on the hunt is the world in which I live too. There is only one world.

Sometimes, while I have stood listening to the owl's auguring song drifting through the trees, when it is ten degrees above nothing and life for any small creature is hard enough without *that,* I have found myself think-ing of summer fields. Fields full of flowers—poppies or lupines. Or, here, fields where the roses hook into the dunes, and their increase is manyfold. All summer they are red and pink and white tents of softness and nectar, which wafts and hangs everywhere—a sweetness so palpable and excessive that, before it, I'm struck, I'm taken, I'm conquered, I'm washed into it, as though it was a river, full of dreaming and idleness—I drop to the sand, I can't move; I am restless no more; I am replete, supine, finished, filled to the last edges with an immobilizing happiness. And is this not also ter-rible? Is this not also frightening?

Are the roses not also—even as the owl is—excessive? Each flower is small and lovely, but in their sheer and silent abundance the roses become an immutable force, as though the work of the wild roses was to make sure that all of us, who come wandering over the sand, may be, for a while, struck to the heart and saturated with a simple happiness. Let the mind be teased by such *stretches* of the imagination, by such balance. Now I am cringing at the very sound of the owl's dark wings opening over my head— not long ago I could do nothing but lounge on the sand and stare into the cities of the roses.

I HAVE TWO FEATHERS from the big owl. One I found near Round Pond; the other, on another day, fell as I watched the bird rise from one tree and flap into another. As it rose, some crows caught sight of it, and so began another scrimmage in their long battle. The owl wants to sleep, but the crows pursue it and when it settles a second time the crows—now a dozen— gather around and above it, and scream into its face, with open beaks and wagging tongues. They come dangerously close to its feet, which are huge and quick. The caught crow is a dead crow. But it is not in the nature of crows to hide or cower—it is in their nature to gather and to screech and to gamble, in the very tree where death stares at them with molten eyes. What fun, to aggravate the old bomber! What joy, to swipe at the tawny feathers even as the bird puffs and hulks and hisses.

But finally the owl rises from the trees altogether and climbs and floats away, over two or three hills, and the crows go off to some other merriment.

And I walk on, over the shoulder of summer and down across the red-dappled fall; and, when it's late winter again, out through the far woodlands of the Provincelands, maybe another few hundred miles, looking for the owl's nest, yes, of course, and looking at everything else along the way.

DEPARTURE

SEAN HILL

# One Saturday Morning

It was spring in Carmel. There were birds. It always
feels like spring in Carmel. It still felt like deep winter
back home in Fairbanks. There were Bushtits and Band-tailed
Pigeons, Acorn Woodpeckers, Western Scrub-Jays
and a Brown Creeper, Black Phoebes, Spotted and California
Towhees, a Townsend's Warbler, and others; a gull floated
high overhead. I stood on the patio in the least layers
I'd worn in months. I held you, legs wrapped by my right arm,
between my wrist and elbow your seat. You'd only recently begun
pointing out the living room window at trucks and cars moving along
the hardpack snow on the road back home. There were birds—
a whole new community for you—and the American Crow
on the wire was the largest, and so I thought the easiest
for your young eyes to perceive, so I pointed up at it, and you
pointed with me with what was surely my hand when
I was your age, but your eyes didn't follow our fingers.
They looked to me and out and inward like when we
listened to music in the kitchen back home in Fairbanks
with our waving hands in the air, but on the patio there
was no music save birdsong. I pulled my hand back
and jabbed it at the crow, and we're doing an old disco move.
I leaned back with you in my arm and watched your eyes
roll down in your head to stay level to the horizon.
After a couple of tries the crow cawed and ruffled its feathers
at us, and you discovered it. O, your emphatic finger showing me
that there was a crow on the wire—acknowledging that bird
and then others. You revealed not what I knew—that there
were birds one Saturday morning in Carmel—but made me feel
again how the world opens before a curious body—our bodies.

Emily Raboteau

# Spark Bird

*Bearing witness to New York's endangered species*

I

F I CAN BE CALLED a bird-watcher, my spark was a pair of burrowing owls, painted on the narrow storefront gate of a shuttered real estate business on 145th Street in Harlem that brokers single-room occupancy housing for two hundred dollars a week. I spotted them after ice-skating with one of my kids at the rink in the shadow of towering smokestacks at Riverbank State Park. The park is a concession to the community for the massive wastewater sewage plant hidden beneath it. It was midway through the Trump years: January, but not cold like Januaries when I was little, not cold enough to see your breath. It wasn't snowing, and it wasn't going to snow. The owls watched me quizzically with their heads cocked, their long skinny legs perched on the colored bands of a psychedelic rainbow that seemed to lead off that gray street into another, more magical realm.

Among people who watch birds, it's often the case that a first bird love, the so-called "spark bird," draws them forever down the bright and rambling path of birding. For Aimee, it was the peacocks in her grandmother's backyard in southern India. For Kerri, it was a whooper swan above Inch Island, Donegal, the year the peace process began. For Windhorse, it was the Baltimore orioles flitting about in the high branches of poplars at his grandfather's house up north on the lake. For Meera, it was the red-winged blackbird, there at the feeder, when she was small. Her mom told her the name and it all clicked into place—*black bird, red wings*—as she learned the game of language and how we match it to the world around us.

I pointed out the extraordinary owls, stopping to take a picture with the camera of my phone.

"Look," I said.

"I want hot cocoa," my kid replied.

We turned the corner and made our way up Broadway toward the Chipped Cup for overpriced Belgian hot chocolate. On the corner of 149th I spotted another bird, the American redstart. It was painted on the security gate of Washington Heights Pediatrics—the kind of doctors' office that struggles to keep the lights on with trifling Medicaid payments and nebulizes asthmatic Black and brown kids, like mine, with albuterol when their lungs constrict too severely for a pump to clear at home. The tuck of color under its wing matched my kid's unnecessary winter hat. I took another picture. Oh New York!—you gorgeous aviary of madcap design. Across the street, in the corner of my eye, were more: a pair of Calliope hummingbirds painted mid-flight outside the Apollo Pharmacy.

That's when I understood there was a pattern.

## II

AFTER THE SPARK, I started noticing scores of them along my two-mile walk to work at City College. Most of the bird murals in Upper Manhattan are spray-painted on the rolled-down gates of mom and pop shops along the gallery of Broadway, at street level. Others are painted up higher on the sides of six-story apartment buildings. Nesting, perching, roosting in the doorways of delis, pharmacies, and barbershops. Lewis's woodpecker at the Taqueria; the almighty boat-tailed grackle at the Buena Vista Vision Center; Brewer's blackbird at the La Estrella dry cleaner, and so on—dozens of bird murals, each one marked in a corner with the name of the ongoing series to which they belong: the Audubon Mural Project.

John James Audubon, the pioneering ornithologist and bird artist, once lived in the hood. He's buried in the cemetery of Trinity Church at 155th Street, midway between my apartment building in Washington Heights and my job in West Harlem, where I teach writing, sometimes using Wallace Stevens's "Thirteen Ways of Looking at a Blackbird" as a prompt. Audubon Terrace, once part of his estate, is now the site of a complex of cultural buildings. Other uptown locales named after Audubon include a housing project, an avenue, and the ballroom where Malcolm X was killed. Its historic facade remains as cladding to a newer medical research building—a concession to Black Americans who protested the ballroom's demolition—at 165th Street, across from the emergency room of NewYork-Presbyterian Hospital. When you walk by these places, as I do, you can spy many of the same birds Audubon chronicled in his masterful archetype of wildlife illustration, *Birds of America* (1827–1838), in the guise of public art.

The project is an unfolding environmental awareness partnership between the gallerist Avi Gitler, the National Audubon Society, and local business and property owners. The murals are sponsored through donations to Audubon and painted by myriad artists, some of them local, in a diverse range of styles. There are presently 148, and counting, bird species depicted uptown. Sometimes they disappear when businesses change hands. The project aims to reach 389. This is the number of North American species, according to Audubon's 2019 *Survival by Degrees* birds and climate report, at risk of extinction from climate change—an alarming two-thirds of North American birds. I have attempted, so far, to photograph them all.

A printable map on the Audubon Society's website indicates the address of each mural. I prefer not to use that resource as a guide. I like the element of surprise. As with actual birders, I never know which birds I'll see on a walk. Sometimes a new bird appears to have landed overnight. Older birds may be marked with graffiti or sullied by weather and grime. I was saddened to discover from the window of the M4 bus while riding downtown that someone had spray-painted over the tundra swan I'd come to love with a cloudy white cipher of bubble letters. Who did that? I wondered, thinking of that rogue graffiti artist known as Spit in the 1984 hip hop movie *Beat Street*, who defaced the work of other artists by tagging over it.

I felt glad to have documented the tundra swan before it disappeared. If temperatures rise three degrees Celsius, 93 percent of this bird's breeding habitat in the tundra of far northern Canada is projected to be lost. Because the Arctic is warming faster than anywhere else on the planet, tundra swans have nowhere farther north to go.

## III

As A PHOTOGRAPHER I am drawn to the visual echoes between the fashion and the feathers, the postures of people and wildlife. For example, the sweep of a dark trench coat that seems to give motion to the peregrine falcon's wings. Or the pair of black track pants that have merged with the legs of the glossy ibis so that the young man wearing them appears to be riding the bird. I wish to document the tensions between human, bird, art, and commercial signage. Sometimes the artists play with these elements, too, as with Snoeman's *Goose Gets Down*, where the bird beneath the canopy of a shoe store is styled in a pair of Timberland boots.

I understand the project has landed in this neighborhood as the site for its campaign because of its connection to Audubon, and also because of the millions of endangered birds that migrate above Manhattan and continue to nest within it. I also appreciate its potential for helping connect a low-income community of color to the green sector, which is predominantly white.

Amelia Earhart is quoted in the mural at Manuel's grocery at 152nd Street: "No borders, just horizons. Only freedom." The bright yellow breast of the mangrove cuckoo pictured there matches the tank of the blowtorch in the hand of the plumber passing by. That bird is described as "a rare bird native to Dominican Republic, Puerto Rico, and the U.S." Unlike nations preoccupied with immigration, the artist states, "Birds See No Borders."

I love these birds for their beauty, the way birders love actual birds, for the exalted brushstrokes of their wingspans that lift us from the drudge of survival. Some birds are reclusive. For example, the Florida scrub jay and Mexican jay have long been trapped behind a hunter green construction fence. The birds on buildings under scaffolding look caged. At businesses that struggle to pay escalating rents by staying open for twelve hours a day, seven days a week, the birds can be seen at night only when the gates come down. At shops that have closed and not yet reopened, like the beauty salon with the laughing gull, the bird is always there.

"We know that the fate of birds and people are intertwined," *Audubon* magazine's editor in chief, Jennifer Bogo wrote me. "That's especially true in communities, like Northern Manhattan, that suffer disproportionately from environmental and human health burdens. We hope that the Audubon Mural Project makes people literally stop in the streets and consider what's at stake with this critically important planetary crisis, while at the same time beautifying and drawing attention to neighborhoods that have historically not been the focus of environmental protections."

To my eye, the project is at once a meditation on impermanence, seeing, climate change, environmental justice, habitat loss, and a sly commentary on gentrification, as many of the working-class passersby are being pushed out of the hood in a migratory pattern that signals endangerment. Most of all, the murals bring me wonder and delight. I can hardly be called a bird-watcher. But because this flock has landed where I live, work, parent, pray, vote, and play, permit me to be your guide.

IV

HERE'S WHAT I can tell you about the Wilson's warbler, which I photographed at a storefront church called Iglesia de Dios El Refugio. They typically avoid the interior of the dense forest, preferring scrubby overgrown clearings and thin woods, staying low in semi-open areas, breeding as far north as timberline, in thickets, second growth, bogs, along wooded streams, moist tangles, low shrubs, groves of willows, and alders near ponds. They nest from coast to coast in Canada but are far more common in the West. In the Rockies and westward, Wilson's warblers are often the most abundant migrants in late spring. Their young are fed by both parents but brooded by the female alone. Their diet consists mostly of insects including bees, beetles, caterpillars, aphids, and also some berries and spiders. Eight to thirteen days after hatching, young warblers leave the nest. Their nest is usually on the ground, often at the base of shrubs, sunken in sedges or moss, shaped like an open cup made of dead leaves and grass, lined with fine grass and hair. If global warming keeps apace, 61 percent of its range will be lost.

Here's what I can tell you about my habitat in Northern Manhattan. I nest in a three-room apartment with my mate and my young on the sixth floor of a mid-rise apartment building around the corner from a commuter bus terminal run by the Port Authority and one block from the on-ramp to the George Washington Bridge, in a neighborhood choked by poverty and highways: the Trans-Manhattan Expressway, Henry Hudson Parkway, and Harlem River Drive. We talked to our young at seven and nine years old, after the murder of George Floyd, about how to protect themselves from the police, who disproportionately apprehend Black and brown youth in our habitat. Among our kind, this grim warning is known as "The Talk." Our diet includes Chinese takeout from The Great Wall, roast chicken from Malecon, and pupusas from Mi Paso Centroamericano. On Halloween, our young eat candy they forage by trick-or-treating from the mom and pop shops along the business thoroughfare of Broadway. Across the street from the bus terminal is the church where we married, and baptized our young, and where an undocumented woman took refuge for months with her American-born children as part of the sanctuary movement, to avoid deportation to Guatemala by federal immigration agents.

Two blocks north of the Wilson's warbler mural on Amsterdam Avenue sits an office of WE ACT for Environmental Justice, an organization that empowers low-income people of color to advocate for healthy communities. It is well documented that some of the most polluted environments in the nation are where people of color live, work, play, and pray. For instance, a 2016 environmental health report on Northern Manhattan by WE ACT stated that, as a result of risks, including poor air quality from heavy diesel truck traffic, dirty boilers, power generation plants, and polluting municipal infrastructure like bus depots and sewage treatment plants, Harlem has a childhood asthma hospitalization rate six times the national and three times the citywide average. A 2017 report from the NAACP and the Clean Air Task Force showed that Black Americans are 75 percent more likely than other Americans to live in fenceline communities sited near facilities producing hazardous waste. A 2018 study by the EPA's National Center for Environmental Assessment found that regardless of their income level, Black Americans are exposed to higher levels of air pollution than white Americans—1.5 times as much of the pollution from burning fossil fuels as the population at large.

I am the mother of Black children in America. It's not possible for me to consider the threats posed to birds without also considering the threats posed to us.

## V

YUMI RODRIGUEZ's grandfather used to call her Colibri. That was his pet name for her: Hummingbird. *Vuela, vuela, Colibri!* he would tell her, encouraging her to fly. She was raised by her grandparents on 161st Street and Broadway across the street from the spot where she would later paint a mural in tribute to her grandfather. Like a lot of immigrants, Odalis Alvarez did a lot of things. He was a clockmaker. A blacksmith. A jewelrymaker. A barber. An artist. And eventually, a business owner. He owned a chain of barbershops in the hood. Yumi describes him as her support network, a quiet person, "a wise, cool dude" with whom she watched nature documentaries.

Yumi went on to get a degree in animal nursing and now works as a veterinary technician to put herself through art school at Cooper Union, where she's pursuing public art. When Yumi's mentor, who does anatomical illustration at the American Museum of Natural History, learned she lived in Washington Heights, he told her about the Audubon Mural Project and put her in touch with Avi Gitler. By this time, her beloved grandfather had grown ill. Yumi reached out to Avi to say she wished to paint a hummingbird—*un colibri*. He showed her the list of available species that hadn't yet been represented. That's how she chose the rufous hummingbird to paint on the gate of Romulo Barber Shop, the last place her grandfather worked. But really, she says, the bird chose her. Serendipitously, she'd read about the rufous hummingbird in a magazine that called it "the toughest bird on the block," with a furious heartbeat and one of the longest migratory journeys for a bird its size, from Mexico to Alaska, following a route of nectar-filled seasonal blooms.

"My grandfather always said I'd persevere," she says. "I share that characteristic with this little bird." She took care when designing her mural that it was "not just a pretty thing," but rather, an image for people to spectate with a sense of respect. She included insects and plants, pollinators integral to the balance of the ecosystem to keep it from collapse. She also included this text: *"Un homenaje a mi abuelo, Odalis Alvarez, por su passion por la conservacion de la naturaleza."*

Yumi's grandfather never got to see the mural. He died of prolonged heart failure in the spring of 2020, when New York City's soundtrack was dominated by two remarkable strains of music: birdsong and sirens.

## VI

DURING LOCKDOWN, traffic dried up on the George Washington Bridge. Without the usual car fumes, the air uptown grew impossibly clear. The din of street life died. New Yorkers with money cleared out for their second homes. It was eerily quiet, and empty. Except for the bodegas, all the storefronts closed. For the first time, I was able to spot the three warblers on the shuttered gate of Monarch Cleaners—a small consolation in the midst of chaos. Prior to the pandemic, that store was always open for business. Nobody had reason for dry cleaning now.

Nine of the ten Manhattan zip codes with the most COVID-19 cases were located uptown. The deaths were proportionate to the same demographic vulnerable to environmental racism—that is, the Black and brown poor. Let me tell you how it was. The shriek of ambulances was incessant. The medical director of a local ER committed suicide, unable to take the strain. The hospital across from the Audubon Ballroom was besieged. The dead were being forklifted into refrigerated trucks.

The murals of remembrance to the birds in my neighborhood were quickly becoming the backdrop to a grief I was yet to figure out how to grasp, much less memorialize: the lopsided COVID deaths among the Black and brown poor in environmentally hazardous zip codes such as ours. Bird-watching is a way of bearing witness—of being transported by the beauty in nature. I'm yanked from that reverie, knowing that Blackness is not a beauty that everyone sees; some see danger, and so my watching is always tenuous, provisional, unstable.

Through biological happenstance, the peak of the pandemic overlapped with the peak of the spring migration of birds along the superhighway of the Atlantic Flyway. While the city's hospitals ran out of beds, staff, and ventilators, the birds stopped by for berries and seeds to fatten themselves on their northward journey. We could hear them clearly in that uncanny pause, filling the air with song. The plaintive call of the white-throated sparrow: "Sam Peabody... Peabody... Peabody." The red-winged blackbird: "Cock-a-r-e-e-e." The ospreys' high-pitched "Killy, killy, killy." The chirruping phrase of the scarlet tanager, "Chick-burr." And the soft sad coo of the mourning dove.

Into this spectacle of avian sound, New York City Audubon Society board member Christian Cooper stepped out with a pair of binoculars at Central Park's Ramble on the morning of May 25—Memorial Day. A morning looking at birds in what is supposed to be a protected wild could quickly become a dangerous encounter where one's serenity is revoked by prejudice. "I'm calling the cops. I'm gonna tell them there's an African American man threatening my life," Amy Cooper (no relation) threatened after he asked her to leash her dog, as per park rules. The National Audubon Society, on whose board Chris Cooper serves, has as its aim to protect birds and the places they need, today and tomorrow. But who will protect those who are watched with suspicion? Who will conserve those of us who need conserving?

That same day, in Minneapolis, George Floyd was killed by police. The video went viral on Twitter: Officer Derek Chauvin pressing his knee on George Floyd's neck for more than eight excruciating minutes, even as he

TORONTO

repeated, "I can't breathe," while horrified onlookers begged for mercy. These two news stories intertwined in the zeitgeist of a pandemic already revealing gross inequities in public health. As Black Lives Matter protests erupted across the nation, institutions that had not previously addressed racial justice as crucial to their missions responded with official public anti-racism statements, nature conservation organizations among them. Audubon's statement on the incident in Central Park begins, "Black Americans often face terrible daily dangers in outdoor spaces, where they are subjected to unwarranted suspicion, confrontation, and violence. The outdoors—and the joy of birds—should be safe and welcoming for all people."

My God, the peculiar American insanity of this statement of the obvious. How outrageous that it needs saying at all.

PROTECT BLACK PEOPLE. COVID-19 somebody spray-painted on a mailbox near our building. At times it feels our desecration is wholesale. I could describe what it sounds like when my children can't breathe. Or the scene, after a police raid, when my son asked me to stop walking the city, out of fear I may be shot. But Black pain is not so cheap. And Black joy is not so rare. I would rather you know that the day I took the M4 bus and wondered who had tagged the tundra swan, I was on my way to pick up free seedling kits for my children from the Horticultural Society of New York, so that we could grow pea shoots in the living room window of our apartment, through which we enjoy watching pigeons and the occasional red-tailed hawk. I would rather imagine the bird Chris Cooper was after that day in the Ramble. Maybe the black-throated green warbler, high in the overstory, calling "Zoo-zoo-zee-zoo"!?

## VII

THE BIRDS BECAME integral to my orientation in the city. I couldn't tell you the exact cross street of the Municipal Credit Union ATM location where I and other city workers withdraw cash, but I could tell you it's right next to the American bald eagle.

One pre-pandemic night after a book party at Alianza Dominicana on 166th Street, I took two friends on an impromptu guided walking tour down Broadway to show them the birds. Kamila lit a joint. By the time we reached the oversize mural of the swallow-tailed kite and other birds at the gas station on the corner of 155th, she was high. I expected her and Aisha to be as enchanted with the birds as I was, but the more of them we encountered, the more edgy Kamila became. She said she felt like she was in Hitchcock's *The Birds*, being watched, under attack. The number of birds was alarming to her. She felt increasingly surrounded.

The weed could have been making her paranoid, warping her perception. But as we approached the pinyon jay over Manny's Restaurant and Lounge near 151st, Aisha, who had never seen the birds and was perfectly sober, said she agreed with Kamila—there was something sinister about them. The murals seemed to her like flags planted by an outside entity, laying claim to the neighborhood.

Aisha's uneasy feeling had to do with real estate. Habitat loss. She suspected the birds had landed to invite or delight an incoming class of people with more money than the people who'd lived here for a long time. Hipsters. White folks. The kind of people who stencil birds on their coffee cups, make noise complaints, and drive up rents. The word she was searching for is "artwashing"—a pattern by which developers identify a neighborhood flourishing with art galleries as having potential for major profit, or in some cases, as with Goldman Properties in Miami using terms like "urban renewal," finance public art projects, like Wynwood Walls, as a driver of such transformation.

Closer to home, in Bushwick, Brooklyn, Mi Casa No Es Su Casa is an organization focused on protecting tenants' rights and affordable housing. It has actively protested against artwashing for pricing people out of the neighborhood—specifically, against mural collaborations between artists and real estate developers in the Bushwick Collective. Would this bird colony contribute to the displacement and ultimate cultural erasure of residents with deep-seated roots? Aisha similarly wondered.

I know this is not the intent of the project, which means instead to connect birds to the local community. Yet in the context of the neighborhood, I can understand such suspicions. I also appreciate that the murals, like all art, may suggest multiple meanings. But then Kamila spotted a bird at the C-Town and started to laugh. It was the black tern, cartoonishly depicted in whooshy lines and candy bright colors. A birder would scratch her head at the illogical rendering. It looks nothing like the black tern. The mural is silly and fanciful, like something one of my children would scribble for fun. We observed its transgression. The bird had broken the second dimension to fling its color onto the tie-dye T-shirt of the oblivious man beside it. It made us indescribably happy. Some works of street art can do this for us—spark joy. So can birds. They bend the straight line, startling us out of our ruts with their riotous colors. When we notice them, they show us patterns.

## VIII

AVI GITLER's partners were interested in creating a dialogue about climate justice, he told me in a larger conversation about the aims of the Audubon Mural Project, but that was not his goal. Personally, he wanted to put up great art, intending to reach kids. "My dream is that twenty-five years from now, an ornithologist will reach out to me to say they grew up in the neighborhood and were turned on to birds by the murals."

Avi, a great-grandchild of Jewish refugees to Washington Heights from Europe, grew up in the neighborhood himself, in the 1990s when it was rough. His grandparents, born in the Heights, were kosher caterers. He attended the local Yeshiva University and its associated high school. With no formal background in the art world except for an education from the Met and the city's other great art museums, he started an art business that led to the establishment of Gitler & _____ gallery on Broadway in 2014. It was the only commercial art business in the neighborhood. He felt jazzed about participating in revitalizing the neighborhood, attracting patrons who would shop in local stores and eat in local restaurants. He chose the location, in part, for its proximity to Audubon Terrace, where, he says, "you can see world-class art for free at the Hispanic Society Museum—probably the only place where you could steal a Velázquez if you spent an hour thinking about how you were going to do it." He got permission from the neighboring store for an artist to paint a flamingo. Then a resident who worked at the Audubon Society noticed the bird, and told Avi about the climate report. Soon after, the mural project began.

The project has the approval of the community board and partnerships with local schools, such as the Washington Heights Expeditionary Learning School. (The fox sparrow was recently painted on an entrance to the school, in honor of its dedicated Environmental and Climate Science teacher, Dr. Jared Fox, who wants to develop a green corridor.) Several uptown artists were commissioned to contribute, including Yumi Rodriguez, and BlusterOne, who lives on 151st. BlusterOne painted the American redstart, for which they named a cocktail at the Harlem Public bar, and more recently, *Three Little Birds*, in honor of Bob Marley, which Avi described as "a positive message in an age of carnage." Avi distinguished the project from the Wynwood Walls in Miami, a public mural project directed by a real estate entity to transform a blighted industrial warehouse district into what the *Miami Herald* described as a lucrative "red-hot residential zone with artistic soul." In Avi's view, the Audubon Mural Project is mindful of the history of street art, "trying to give voice to the voiceless. Who has more ultimate lack of agency than a population of birds?" He cited the AIDS era and work of Keith Haring as its origin, appearing "where nobody wanted to go."

Now there are tours of the Harlem murals on Sunday mornings, offered through the Audubon Society of New York, for thirty dollars a head.

## IX

I FIRST MET Karen Taylor years ago at an exhibit of the family photos of her husband, whose Harlem roots extend eight generations. Karen is founder and executive director of While We Are Still Here. According to its website, the nonprofit organization formed as "a response to the threat that each building's history would be lost and gone forever, partially due to the passing of time, and partially due to 'gentrification,' which is rapidly altering the environment." Before the wrecking ball of displacement demolishes community memory, Karen aims to codify it, while we are still here, so more people can learn how ordinary Black migrants, primarily from the South, sought refuge from domestic terror and wound up transforming Harlem into a global center of intellectual, artistic, and political influence.

While We Are Still Here is dedicated to the preservation of Harlem's Black history, particularly as it played out in two historic buildings on Edgecombe Avenue, 409 (where Karen lives) and 555. Luminary residents of these addresses in the early and mid-twentieth century included W.E.B. DuBois, Walter White, James Weldon Johnson, Thurgood Marshall, Joe Louis, Paul Robeson, and Count Basie—though Karen is quick to point out that regular folks lived there too: beauticians, musicians, and gangsters alike. She believes their collective legacy of fighting inequality leaves a blueprint for our current struggles. I believe she is right.

"Many people seem to have no idea that this community was full of involved and evolved people who lived, worked, thrived, and engaged in activities such as seeing to it that their children were educated, curating art shows in church basements and storefronts or on the sidewalk, and coaching Little League teams, as well as offering instruction in the various art forms," began Karen when I asked her how she felt about the birds. It struck me that she was speaking about our community in the past tense. Her impulse to preserve its history ran parallel to the mural project.

Unlike me, Karen wasn't a fan of the bird project. Normally outspoken, she had difficulty articulating why she felt provoked by it. It wasn't so much that its namesake was "a slave-owning white nationalist," as she'd learned during her time working for *Audubon* magazine, but that this tribute to his legacy was unfolding now, when Black people in Harlem were being displaced. She allowed that the project might be fueled by someone else's idea of beauty. To her, the birds' faces were frightening. "They all look like raptors," she said, referring to the same five-story mural by Lunar New Year that bugged out Kamila. Furthermore, Karen took umbrage with the proprietor of a new café called the Monkey Cup who said she liked the project because it offered kids something beautiful to look at—as though beauty was lacking before the birds showed up.

There's nothing wrong with sounding the alarm that birds are suffering because of climate change, Karen concluded—but if she had the funding, she'd pay artists to commemorate the Lenape people of the region displaced by European expansionism, and the Black people who made Harlem.

## X

*Let us imagine the servant ordered down on all fours*
*In the manner of an ottoman whereupon the boss volume*
*Of John James Audubon's "Birds of America" can be placed.*

Terrance Hayes offers this image of casual violence in his poem, "Antebellum House Party." An absurd degradation. The Black body as a prop. The problem with the picture is that it's so easy for us to imagine. Easier than it is to imagine a sky without birds.

## XI

ON AMSTERDAM and 163rd Streets, ten blocks from Karen's building is one of the Audubon Mural Project's boldest works: *Endangered Harlem*. Painted by street artist Gaia, it takes up the entire facade of an apartment block. This mural includes four species of migratory songbirds: the black-and-white warbler, magnolia warbler, scarlet tanager, and tree swallow (passerines, all). In the top right corner Gaia painted a portrait of John James Audubon as a young man; in the bottom right, a photo by Russell Lee taken in the South Side of Chicago in 1941, during the swell of the Second Great Migration; in the bottom left, the hand of James Lancaster, who led the East India Company's first fleet in 1600, resting on a globe.

"I'm grateful to be able to be a part of the Audubon Mural Project and to have had the opportunity to push this Photoshop method of arranging history visually," Gaia shares on Audubon's website. "These three patterns of migration run parallel to one another. But the greatest irony of it all is raising ecological awareness whilst the people of Harlem are endangered of significant gentrification."

I felt that irony while shooting the great gray owl, by the artist Key Detail, one of my favorite bird murals. I wanted to document it before it was gone. I stood there a long time in front of the Daliza Pharmacy, trying to frame the shot to put a person on an equal plane. "You gonna buy this building?" a man confronted me. He was missing some teeth, looked in rough shape, maybe unsheltered. He'd known the owner, he said, back in the day. He felt bewildered by the changes, like at the Chipped Cup: a fishbowl full of white people, as he put it. "No," I told him, "I just like the bird." He considered the owl, and spat on the sidewalk. "Fucking birds," he cursed.

## XII

BROOKLYN-BASED studio artist George Boorujy, who painted *Gang of Warblers* on Dibond with outdoor house paints, wanted to depict them as a bunch of tough guys because they make massive migration journeys, some inconceivable for creatures so small. He also hung two other billboard-size warbler paintings over the subway entrance at 157th Street, a difficult installation performed on a lift in the middle of the night in winter, ripping down calcified signage for a drink called "Energy 69." From that vantage he witnessed the Rockefeller Christmas tree being driven down Broadway.

When I asked George why he was drawn to warblers, he said, "I feel as though warblers in particular can be important ambassadors for conversation, like a gateway drug." He's noticed it's often the spring migration of warblers, especially in the eastern U.S., that gets people interested and then hooked on bird-watching. "This curiosity leads to learning about these birds, and the first step to caring about something is knowing about it. The fact that these birds live in multiple countries also encourages a broader view of conservation. If a birder in Ohio wants to see the return of 'their' warblers, they have to also be invested in preserving habitat in Central and South America and the Caribbean."

There are 3 billion fewer birds in the U.S. and Canada than fifty years ago. That's a staggering 29 percent. We know this because of the bird-watchers who, having caught the spark, and out of devotion, submit their observations to databases and help carry out population surveys year after year.

Conservationists say the birds are dying because of pesticides, habitat loss, urbanization, and development, as with glass-clad high-rise buildings like the Circa, on the corner of 110th and Central Park West, in front of which, especially during migration season, dozens of bird carcasses can be found each morning on the sidewalk after window strikes. Some researchers point to climate change. In fall 2019, scientists reported a mass die-off of up to a million migratory birds across the U.S. Southwest and Mexico, many with little muscle mass, seeming to have dropped dead from the sky mid-flight, like the proverbial canaries in a coal mine. At the time, wildfires were considered a factor. Of the disappearing birds, warblers are among the worst hit groups, and therefore, the most commonly represented in the murals. Their population has declined by 617 million in the last half century.

George feels the barrier of entry to bird-watching, and thus a connection to wildlife, is low. I'm not sure that's the case, though I want it to be. In his view, one doesn't have to go to a national park or a far-flung part of the planet to see them. They are everywhere. And one's connection and concern for them leads one to care about environmental issues everywhere. "Our birds are their birds too. It's all connected," he says.

## XIII

I REACHED the corner of 135th Street and Amsterdam to watch Marthalicia Matarrita, in her paint-splattered pants, finish making the gray hawk. It was November, the saddest month. Even from across the street, the mural's lush green background suggested treetops. I saw the finely barred chest pattern, the rounded wings, the hooked beak, and the magnificent thing Marthalicia had done. She had taken the bird out of the sky to ground in our midst. And she had elevated us to its height. The hawk was about to land: talons reaching sharply for the perch, gaze intent, tail feathers spread for balance.

Marthalicia was slightly rattled. An old man she knew from the church she used to attend on 133rd had just confronted her, demanding to know: "Are you making this for us or for them?"

That was the wrong question. At the base of Marthalicia's stepladder were $140 worth of spray paint cans. This was her second go at the hawk, which she chose, in part, because it reminded her of her mother's gray hair. In her first version, the bird was already perched on the branch. But too much white space was left on the wall, and she worried it would get tagged over. So she redid it with its wings spread, working from a photograph.

Marthalicia grew up in the neighborhood in a string of apartments in what she describes as the "Harlem band," stretching from the west side to the east. Sharp life turns moved her family from one place to the next. They were evicted from 137th and Riverside. For a time they lived on 145th. Her interest in art made her an outlier. "I'm not artistically supported by my family or my community," she said. The sharp turns continued. She went to SUNY New Paltz to study art, having joined the Army Reserve to pay for school, but was yanked from her studies by a call to Kuwait and a pregnancy. Now, age forty-two, she lives with her two children in a basement apartment in the Bronx, without room to make work, except outside. It's what she can afford.

Birds, in Marthalicia's view, are spiritual messengers. She too noticed a pattern. Before a friend or family member would die, she'd see a dead pigeon. Or after someone passed, she'd see white feathers and wonder if it was a sign. "When you're from the city, you look down. You don't call attention to yourself, especially as a woman. You keep your guard up. Nobody looks at the sky." But birds, she felt, were trying to tell her something.

Sometimes they'd land near her. Crows. Hawks. Gulls. Previously, all she'd been aware of were water bugs, roaches, rats, and pigeons. Remembering the big earthquake in Haiti in 2010, when animals were attuned to the vibrations of oncoming disaster before people, she asked, "and *we're* supposed to be more advanced?"

The artist shakes the can of white. Its bead rattles. She holds the printed picture of the gray hawk up against the wing she's made on the wall, using the paper's edge to make short straight white lines with the spray paint. The mural is beginning to look real. She lingers on the flight feathers. Then she stops. Looks up. Points out the hawk circling above the building at City College where I teach writing. Her face is a picture of awe.

She tells me it's the anniversary of her mother's death. The hawk is doing what hawks do. Together, we watch her painting the sky.

ALISON HAWTHORNE DEMING

# Refuge

Glossy ibis, says the guide, setting her tripod
on pavement, training the lens for the birdwatchers
to fix the downward-curved bill and spindly legs
of the wader. I can't help but itch
to get closer than this tailored birdwalk. Once

I rode to low marshland with a friend. The horses
mucking up to their knees, parting the brushy alders
where there wasn't any trail. We gave them their heads,
trusting their instincts to get to dry land.
On the far side we rested, the woods

glowing with rust and lemon. We sat. Reins dropped,
the horses leaned to fidget the leaves.
Wind thickened in the evergreens. Then the quiet
        cracked—
wings that loud slapped the air—brittle legs
arrowed through weeds to land not five feet away.

The great blue heron, eye fired toward shore,
where we held our breath. Even when
we began to speak, edging slightly closer,
she stayed. And something in her lack of fear,
the fix of one black iris on us—horses,

woman and man alike—kept us in our place.

CATHEDRAL 2

WILLIAM STAFFORD

# Malheur Before Dawn

An owl sound wandered along the road with me.
I didn't hear it—I breathed it into my ears.

Little ones at first, the stars retired, leaving
polished little circles on the sky for awhile.

Then the sun began to shout from below the horizon.
Throngs of birds campaigned, their music a tent of sound.

From across a pond, out of the mist,
one drake made a V and said its name.

Some vast animal of air began to rouse
from the reeds and lean outward.

Frogs discovered their national anthem again.
I didn't know a ditch could hold so much joy.

So magic a time it was that I was both brave and afraid.
Some day like this might save the world.

SANDRA STEINGRABER

# The Fall of a Sparrow

*Is* Passer domesticus *the new canary?*

*Where they live*

THEY ARRIVE uninvited, poor relations with little to recommend them and no plans to leave. Their motto: this'll do. A hole or a crevice is fine for them. So are rafters, ivy, a streetlamp, a rain-gutter clip. In Kansas, they reside in the continuously bobbing heads of oil pumps. In Turkmenistan, they excavate loess banks. In the Arctic, they squat in railroad roundhouses. Found on six continents, they are the world's most widely distributed bird. Urban or rural is immaterial to them. Except for this: they are never found more than four hundred meters from a human structure.

*What the evolutionary ecologists say*

They are obligate commensals of *Homo sapiens*. Meaning they cannot live without us. They are our avian shadows. They are Ruth to our Naomi. *Wherever you go, there shall I follow. Your home shall be mine.* They have disembarked from our ships. They have traveled with us along the Trans-Amazonian Highway. In northern Finland, in South Africa, across all of Siberia and the Americas, in the Bahamas, the Azores, the Falklands, and Cape Verde, we cohabitate. No one recalls when the house sparrow gave up the habit of seasonal migration.

*Where they came from*

They did not arrive. They are as old as agriculture, having speciated at about the time we first threw seeds on the ground and settled down. Their fossils have been found in caves near Bethlehem in Palestine and atop Mount Carmel in Israel. It was *Passer domesticus biblicus* to which Jesus was referring when he asked, rhetorically, "Are not two sparrows sold for a farthing?" They are the species God's eye is on. They are believed to have spread to Europe in tandem with the horse.

The answer is probably Iraq.

*What they eat*

Mostly cereal grain and weed seeds. *Preglossale* is the name of the bone embedded in their tongues for husking. Stomach-content studies show a strong preference for millet over fescue. Catholic in their tastes, they switch to insects during the breeding season. They find dinner in the grillwork of automobiles. They rob spiderwebs. In Australia, they flutter before the electronic sensors of automatic doors and thereby gain entry into supermarkets. In Hawai'i, they gather on hotel balconies and await the emergence of honeymooning couples at breakfast hours. In Norwegian winters, they forage in total darkness. They are known to consume baby mice. They dislike eating alone.

*What they say*

Mostly *chirrup*, which the Germans hear as *tshlip* and the British as *phip*. Sonographs reveal other vocalizations not distinguishable to the human ear. Throughout the day, they gather in communal roosts and chatter, presumably about foraging routes.

*Their contributions to science*

Much of what we know about the effect of light-to-dark ratios on sexual maturation comes from experiments using house sparrows, which are not legally protected. For this, they have been hooded, blinded, caged in darkness, castrated, pinealectomized, and defeathered. *Passer domesticus* is the lab rat of the avian world.

*Their world-renowned expert*

He is retired biologist Ted R. Anderson, a man you might wish for your own father. Gregarious, curious, easygoing, Anderson hoped to land a research position after graduate school. Instead, he found himself employed at a teaching college in the soy fields of Illinois. He stayed on, raised a family, and studied sparrows. His life's work is distilled into a 547-page monograph. Nine years in the writing, it brings together literature from all over the world, involves translations from Russian, and contains elegantly drawn graphs accompanied by captions such as "Monthly Changes in the Mean Volume of the Left Testis of a House Sparrow in Iowa." The book's final paragraph is this: "As I watch live television news from Baghdad, Gaza, Jerusalem, or Kosovo and hear sparrows chirping in the background, I sometimes wonder what opinion, if any, the house sparrow has about the havoc wreaked by its human hosts."

*The mystery of their badges*

Males sport a black bib, or badge, that varies considerably in size among individuals. Why? Badge size does not predict dominance. It is not related to command of resources. It is not a function of size or health. Females show no preference for large- or small-badged males. If size matters to the house sparrow, it matters in ways not known to us.

*The mystery of their worldwide disappearance*

Like the honeybee, the house sparrow is experiencing unexplained, catastrophic population collapses, including here in the Americas but especially among urban populations in Europe. Unlike honeybees, sparrows generate few headlines announcing their ongoing demise. In England and Ireland, the number of breeding pairs has declined by 30 to 50 percent over the past two decades, a loss of as many as 7 million birds. In some urban areas, losses approach 99 percent. Says Anderson, "Not since the Irish Potato Famine . . . have the British Isles witnessed such a major population decline." A lowered survival rate among juveniles appears to be the problem. Newly emerging avian diseases? There is some evidence for this hypothesis from Europe. Global climate change? There is some evidence for this hypothesis from Israel. The sparrow is the new canary.

*Autobiography with house sparrow*

The spring my mother's breast cancer returned, I found an injured sparrow on the concrete slab of the school bus stop. I took it home and fed it milk-soaked bits of bread. Eventually, it learned to fly—but never properly because its left leg jutted out at a right angle, so it would flutter around me in loopy circles. Finally, it died. I told my mother it had flown away.

In college, I studied ornithology. My English-major boyfriend, wanting to join me in the spirit of birding, called me to the window of our wretched apartment, excited about the wrens in the hedge. "Those are just house sparrows," I shrugged. "They're invasive. They take over bluebird boxes. They're everywhere."

I have begun searching for them in parking lots, around grain elevators and loading docks, among the landscaping at gas stations, along subway station stairwells, under freeway overpasses. Are these spaces more sparrowless than they used to be? Is there an inanimation among the dirt and dust where, formerly, dirt- and dust-colored inhabitants cocked their heads? Have I taken too little care of this?

On an unusually warm evening, I met a colleague in the courtyard of a downtown restaurant. We looked together at the latest breast cancer statistics. The ivy shivered with sparrows, and their incessant chirping made conversation difficult. An ashen feather fell into my wineglass. I was happy, happy to receive it.

CLEOPATRA MATHIS

# Salt Water Ducks

The tide ignores its limits, all last night
climbing over the railing, battering the door.
White spume flew its ghost against the glass.
The bay's in its third day of outrage,
but the ducks have to eat. The white-winged scoter
keeps me at the window, three sleek ones.
I count the in and out of their pristine heads—
bodies down for improbable minutes
before coming back up, black and white
against the white-capped black water shoving
against the row of stone pilings that mark the tide's high rise.
By 8 a.m. I've seen enough
as the rocks submerge and the overwrought current,
something like a boxer pounding and pounding,
slams the ducks diving there—I've seen enough

to know what I'll find tomorrow on the wasted beach:
a washed-up duck, still intact,
limp sack beneath the flawless design
of its feathers, nothing odd except the crumpled pose.
Audubon propped them up on wires, a scaffold of bird—
no other way to capture life than to show it dead.
Brutality not part of art's equation, we like to think.
Meanwhile, the birds are all instinct
in the moment. This life in a wild wind
is only the din they live in. I doubt they even hear it.

SWIFTEST

LI-YOUNG LEE

# Evening Hieroglyph

Birds keep changing places in the empty tree
like decimals or numerals reconfiguring

some word which, spoken, might sound the key
that rights the tumblers in the iron lock
that keeps the gate dividing me from me.

Late January. The birds face all
one direction and flit
from branch to branch.

They raise no voice
against or for oncoming dark, no answer
to questions asked by one
whose entire being seems a question

posed to himself, one no longer new
on earth, unknowing, and yet,
still not the next thing.

LIA PURPURA

# On Coming Back as a Buzzard

*(If you believe in coming back)*

I KNOW, coming back as a crow is a lot more attractive. If crows and buzzards do the same rough job—picking, tearing, and cleaning up—who wouldn't rather return as a shiny blue crow with a mind for locks and puzzles? A strong voice, and poem-struck. Sleek, familiar, omen-bearing. Full of mourning and ardor and talk. Buzzards are nothing like this, but something other, complicated by strangeness and ugliness. They intensify my thinking. They look prehistoric, pieced together, concerned. I might simply say I feel closer to them—always have—and proceed. Because, really, as I turn it over, the problem I'm working on here, coming back as a buzzard, has not so much to do with buzzards after all.

A buzzard is *expected* at the table. The rush would be over by the time I got there and I, my lateness sanctioned, might rightfully slip in. I wouldn't saunter, nor would I blow in dramatically—*flounce*, as my grandmother would say. The road would be the dinner table (just as the dinner table, with its veering discussions, is always a road somewhere) and others' distraction would resolve—well, I would resolve it—into a clean plate.

I would be missed if I were not there. Not at first, not in the frenzy, but later.

Without me, no outlines, no profiles come clear. The very idea of scaffolding is diminished.

"The smaller scraps are tastier" would have no defender. "Close to the bone" would fall out of use as a measure of sharply felt truth.

Without a chance to walk away from abundance, thus proving their wealth, none of the first eaters would be content with their portion. I make their bestowing upon the least of us possible.

With me around, mishaps—side of the highway, over a cliff, more slowly dispensed by poison—do not have to be turned to a higher purpose. I step in. I make use of.

And here, I'm whittling away at the problem.

As a buzzard, I'd know the end of a thing is precisely not that. Things go on, in their way. My presence making the end a beginning, reinterpreting the idea of abundance, allowing for the ever-giving nature of Nature—I'd know these not as religious thoughts. It's rather that, apportioned rightly, there's always enough, more than enough. "Nothing but gifts on this poor, poor earth," says Milosz, who understood perfectly the resemblance between dissolve and increase. Rain scours and sun burns away excesses of form. And rain also seeds, and sun urges forth fuses of green.

I'd love best the movement of stages and increments, to repeat "this bank and shoal of time" while below me banks and shoals of a body went on welling/receding, rising and dropping. I'd be perched on a wire, waiting, ticking off not the meat reducing, but how what's left, like a dune, shifts and reconstitutes. Yes, it *looks* like I hover, and the hovering, I know, suggests a discomfiting eagerness. Malevolence. Why is that? I haven't killed a thing. If the waiting seems untoward, it may be confirming something too real, too true: all the parts that slip from sight, can't be easily had, collapse in on themselves and require digging, all the parts that promise small, intense bursts of sweetness unnerve us—while the easily abundant, the spans, the expanses (thick haunch, round belly, and shoulder), all that lifts easily to another's lips, and retains its form till the end—seems pure. Right and deserved. Proper and lawful. Thus butchers have their neat diagrams. One knows to call for *chop, loin, shank, rump.*

I'd get to be one who, when passed the plate, seeks first the succulent eye. This would mark me: *foreigner.* Stubborn lover of scraps and dark meat. Base. Trained on want and come to love piecemeal offerings—the shreds and overlooked tendernesses too small for a meal, but carefully, singularly gathered—like brief moments that burst: isolate beams of sun in truck fumes, underside of wrist against wrist, sudden cool from a sewer grate rising. I incline toward the tucked and folded parts (the old country can't be bred out of me), the internals with names that lack correspondence, the sweetbreads and umbles, bungs, hoods, liver-and-lights. If the road is a plate, then the outskirts of fields and settlements where piles are heaped are plates, too. And the gullies, the ditches, the alleys—all plates. I'd get to reorder your thoughts about troves, to prove the spilled and shoveled-aside to be treasure. To reconfer notions of milk and honey, and how to approach the unbidden.

I resemble, as I suppose we all do, the things I consume: bent to those raw flaps of meat, red, torn, cast aside, my head also looks like a leftover thing, chewed. I have my ways of avoiding attention: vomit to turn away predators. Shit, like the elegant stork, on my legs to cool off, to disinfect the swarming microbes I tread daily. I am gentle. And cautious. I ride the thermals and flap very little (*conserve, conserve*) and locate food by smell. I'm a black V in air. A group of us on the ground is a *venue*. In the air we're a *kettle*.

I reuse even the language.

A simple word, *aftermath*, structures my day. Sometimes I think *epic*— doesn't everyone apply to their journey a story? Then *flyblown, feculent, scavenge* come—how it must seem to others—and the frame of my story's reduced. Things are made daily again. The first eaters are furiously driven— by hunger, and brute need releasing trapdoors in the brain. Such push and ambition! I hold things in pantry spots in my body and take out and eat what I've saved when I need it, and so am never furious. On my plate, choice reduces. I take what I come upon, and the work of a breeze cools the bowl's steaming contents. There's a beauty in this singularity: consider bringing to each occasion your one perfect bowl, one neat fork/spoon/knife set. That when the chance comes, you're given to draw the tine-curves between lips, pull, lick, tap clean the spoon's curvature—and for these sensations, there's ample time. Time pinned open, like the core of a long summer afternoon.

Am I happy? Yes, in momentary ways. Which I think is a good way to feel about things that come when they will, and not when you will them. While I'm waiting, I get to be with the light as it shifts off the wet phone wire, catches low sun, holds, pearls and unpearls drops of water. If I bounce just a little, they shiver and fall, and my weight calls more pearls to me. There's light over the blood-matted rib-fur, and higher up, translucing on the still-unripped ear of the fox. Light through drops of fresh resin on pine limbs, light on ditchwater neverminding the murk. I get fixed by spoors of light, silver shine on silks and tassels, light choosing the lowliest, palest blue gristle for lavishing. I wait at a height and from afar, with what looks like a hunch-shouldered burden. Below, the red coils of spilled guts gather dust on the ground. Such a red and its steam in the cold gets to be *shock*—and *riches*. Any red interruption on asphalt, on hillside, at dune's edge—*shock*, and not a strewn thing, not waste. Not a mess. Plump entrails crusting with sage and dirt tighten in sun: piercing *that* is an undersung moment, filled with a tender resistance, a sweetness, slick curves and tangles to dip into, tear, stretch, snap, and swallow.

The problem with coming back as a buzzard is the notion of *coming back*. I can't believe in the coming-back.

Sure, I play the dinnertime game, everyone identifying their animal-soul, the one they choose to reveal their best depth, the one, when the time comes, they hope fate will award them: Strong eagle! Smart dolphin! Joyful golden retriever! But there's the issue of where I'd have to go first, in order to make a return. And the idea of things I did or failed to do in a lifetime fixing the terms of my return—and the keeping of records, and just who's totting it up. As soon as I imagine returning anew (brave-stallion reward, dung-beetle reproach), I lose heart. It's too easy.

Anyway, I already think like a buzzard.

The times I forget my child, most powerfully marked by the moments that follow, in which I abruptly remember him again, with sharp breath, disturbed at the oversight—those times are evidence enough of my fall into reverie, into all that is set, unbidden, before me: inclinations gone to full folds, bone-shaded hollows, easings and slouchings, taut ridges, matched dips, cupped small of the back, back of the neck, the ever-giving body—yes, I take what's set before me. So much feels hosted—and fleet. I chew a little koan: all things go / always more where that came from.

That the world calls me to hissing and grunting, that I am given a nose for decay's weird sweetness, that I am arranged in a broken-winged pose to dry feathers and bake off mites in the sun, that I love the wait, that I have my turn, that no one wants my job so I go on being needed—I have my human equivalences for these.

ROBERT CORDING

# Watching Cranes, I Think of Camus

Tonight, our spoonful of uplift
is red-crowned cranes, wings up,
legs down, floating into the DMZ
on the feel-good spot of the news.

*It's almost a sanctuary*, the reporter says,
*this open, empty land that runs along*
*the 38th parallel between North*
*and South Korea for 160 miles.* It's true,

the cranes have found refuge here,
the land, people-less, littered with mines
and surrounded by troops, left behind
to the birds for the time being.

It's almost comical how the news report
thinks it needs to shuffle between
an opportunistic nature rushing in
to fill an emptiness, and the vague sense

of some power larger than us
fixing once again what we've broken.
I'm no better. I'm dragging up Camus,
who wondered how we could ever be

miserable, so much beauty in the world,
but, also, how we could ever be happy,
so much shit in the world. Yes, Camus
is there, uninvited, in the final montage—

a new day, the morning sun oranging
the snow-dusted marsh, the camera closing in
on a pair of cranes, their necks dipping,
rising, one head bowing to the other until

the pair lift into air as if they are levitating,
then fall, their wings opened like parachutes
as they touch down ever so lightly on the earth
where all that poised firepower waits.

Mariana Gosnell

# The Ice Nursery

*For emperor penguins, a barren ice shelf beneath
the darkness of the Antarctic winter is just the spot
to raise a family*

I T IS THE WORST OF PLACES, the worst of times. The Antarctic coast.
The dead of winter. Temperatures down to minus sixty degrees Fahr-
enheit. Wind speeds up to eighty miles an hour. Darkness around the
clock. "Ground" a slab of sea ice. Yet in that place and at that time, male
emperor penguins stand without shelter or food or drink or breaks for a lie-
down or even much movement for two whole months, holding eggs on top
of their toes. The scene is one of such extremity—thousands of hunched-over
birds being lashed by blizzards—that it suggests something amiss in the ratio-
nal workings of reproductive biology. Is this hardship necessary?

The first people to see a breeding colony of emperor penguins were men
from Robert Scott's Discovery expedition who looked down on one from a
very high precipice at Cape Crozier in the early Antarctic spring (October)
of 1902. When those men reported to their colleagues back at camp that
the penguins had well-developed chicks with them, one colleague, zoolo-
gist Edward Adrian Wilson, remarked that "they must lay their eggs very
early indeed." Almost ten years later, Wilson, Apsley Cherry-Garrard, Scott,
and several other men from the Terra Nova expedition rowed toward Cape
Crozier for another look. This time it was summer in Antarctica (mid-
January). "[A]bout six feet above us on a small dirty piece of the old bay ice
about ten feet square," Wilson wrote in his journal, "one living emperor
penguin chick was standing disconsolately stranded, and close by stood one
faithful old emperor parent asleep." The rest of the penguins had apparently

departed already, "gone north to sea on floating bay ice." Wilson found it "curious" that with all the clean ice around, the "destitute derelicts" should have chosen to stand on the only remaining piece of bay ice, and it filthy. He figured that the penguins were waiting for the ice to carry them out to sea and wondering why it was taking so long.

"Another point was most weird to see," Wilson noted, was "that on the underside of this very dirty piece of sea-ice, which was about two feet thick and which hung over the water as a sort of cave, we could see the legs and lower halves of dead emperor chicks hanging through, and even in one place a dead adult." After Scott himself saw the hanging parts (which he noted included a flipper), he wrote in his journal that the birds "had evidently been frozen in above and were being washed out under the floe."

On finding the single living chick, the explorers guessed why the penguins breed when they do. The chick was "still in the down," Wilson wrote, and if its egg had been laid in summer as the eggs of other species of penguins are, it would still have been in the down—that is, without a protective coat of feathers—when winter arrived. "Thus," Cherry-Garrard concluded in his account of the visit, "the emperor penguin is compelled to undertake all kinds of hardships because his children insist on developing so slowly."

Emperors develop slowly because they are large. They are the largest diving birds in the world, the largest of all eighteen species of penguins, more than twice as large as the next largest species, king penguins. They stand almost three feet high and weigh about ninety pounds. In cold regions, having a large body mass is better than having a small one, since for a given volume there's less surface area from which heat can escape and more room in which insulating fats can be stored. But growth takes time; there's a limit to how fast cells can divide. Biologists now know that it takes six months for an emperor chick to fledge and that the breeding in emperor colonies is timed so the chick is capable of feeding itself when the short summer season begins. Adults therefore have no choice but to court and lay and incubate and hatch their eggs during the long Antarctic night, under the harshest circumstances of any bird—any vertebrate—on Earth.

Cherry-Garrard's book, *The Worst Journey in the World*, recounts the trip that he, Wilson, and Henry R. "Birdie" Bowers took to the rookery at Cape Crozier on foot seven months after they had rowed past it. They went to get some eggs. At that time there was a widespread belief that embryos as they grow pass sequentially through previous stages of the animal's evolution-ary development, and if the penguin embryos had scales on them, as did dinosaurs from which flying birds were believed to have descended, it would demonstrate that penguins are the missing link.

The three men left the expedition's quarters in June, five days after Midwinter Night. "It is midday but it is pitchy dark, and it is not warm," Cherry-Garrard wrote—the last time he would resort to understatement. For the next five weeks, while covering only seventy-six miles, the men endured "cold such as had never been experienced by human beings," temperatures as low as minus seventy-seven and a half degrees Fahren-heit. They had to cross some of the largest pressure ridges in the Antarc-tic, formed by the compression of the four-hundred-mile-long Great Ice Barrier (now called Ross Ice Shelf) against the rocky shoreline. They fell repeatedly into "furrows" fifty or sixty feet deep; struggled around "huge heaps of ice pressed up in every shape on every side, crevassed in every direction"; skirted "great walls of battered ice"; and blundered into a cul-de-sac formed when two ridges of glacial ice "butted on to the sea-ice," as Cherry-Garrard expressed it.

"And then we heard the emperors calling. Their cries came to us from the sea-ice we could not see but which must have been a chaotic quarter of a mile away. They came echoing back from the cliffs, as we stood helpless and tantalized." Their way to the colony was blocked by a pressure ridge that had been thrown "end on" against a cliff, but Wilson discovered a "black hole, something like a fox's earth, disappearing into the bowels of the ice," and they managed to wriggle through it and on emerging stood, "three crystal-lized ragamuffins, above the emperors' home."

Home turned out to be not on the thick ice of the glacial shelf but on the thin sea ice of the bay. There were only about one hundred penguins on it. "[W]here were all the thousands of which we had heard?" they wondered. Nevertheless, the men grabbed five penguin eggs, stuck them inside their fur mitts, and "legged it back as hard as we could go" to the place where they'd left their pickling gear. The journey back was even worse than the journey out had been. At times they thought that death was inevitable, then that death was desirable: "a crevasse seemed almost a friendly gift."

As the only surviving member of the egg expedition (Wilson and Bow-ers died with Scott on the return trek from the South Pole), Cherry-Garrard presented three eggs to custodians of the Natural History Museum in South Kensington, London, who were indifferent, even annoyed, by the donation ("This ain't an egg shop," one said). Eventually, a professor took a look at the embryos and found the rudiments of feathers on them; the penguin was not, after all, the missing link.

FORTY YEARS PASSED before anybody visited a penguin colony in the middle of winter again. Then in 1952, a young Frenchman, Jean Prévost, spent a full year, including "the long night of polar winter," observing 12,500 emperors in a colony at Pointe Geologie in Adélie Land, near a base of the French Polar Expedition. The colony had only recently been discovered by sled-dog trainers out on a practice run. In the doctoral thesis Prévost later wrote, "Ecologie du Manchot Empereur," he described the penguins' breeding cycle, which is tied to the ice cycle. Both last almost ten months and begin in March. Two penguins had already made it up onto the young, flexible sea ice of March without Prévost seeing them, but he did spot the third bird coming in. It approached the other two, lowered its head, and after a few seconds lifted it. One of the other penguins did the same, then stood facing the newcomer for several minutes before turning away. Prévost later realized that he had witnessed the first tentative search for a partner as well as the first "mutual display."

On this icy stage, he was to see many more mutual displays, because emperors perform them in all "social and family circumstances." The face-to-face display, for instance, performed not only when seeking a mate but also after laying an egg, is preceded by a "love song," Prévost reported, a sort of cackle that ends in a short or long note, emitted by one penguin with its head lowered toward the ice, its beak slightly open, and its neck bent like a shepherd's crook. In one variation of that display, after the lowering of heads and bending of necks, one penguin approaches the other in a "balanced walk," stops in front of it, and with its body arched over its feet slowly lifts its head and points its beak toward the sky. This exposes its brood patch, the bare place on the belly of adults against which an egg or newborn chick is placed before a protective flap of feathered skin is draped over it. Standing with their breasts pressed together, or with only a bit of space separating them, the two penguins are in an "ecstatic" state, or so it appeared to Prévost, with their eyelids half closed. The ecstasy doesn't last long before they

FISH HUNTER 3

simultaneously make swallowing movements and relax their bodies. Then they may do it all over again.

As for the "nuptial display," the male shows his brood patch to the female and then inclines his head toward her belly, "as if to observe the egg," Prévost wrote, and touches her belly with his beak. Even at this advanced state of courtship, the female may reject him. Undeterred, he may pass his beak over her neck and invite her to stretch herself out on the ice.

A month later, the female lays a single egg, which is all the male has room for in his brood pouch. She brings her tail forward between her feet, apparently to soften the fall of the egg onto the ice, and upon seeing the egg slide downward, the male sings. No sooner has the egg touched the ice than the female maneuvers it up onto her feet, using her beak. She shows the egg to the male, inclines her head, and sings. He regards the egg and, while groaning slightly and trembling, touches it with his beak. Then he touches the female's brood pouch, looks down at his own brood pouch, becomes agitated and "insistent," pushes the female, and sometimes tries to take the egg from her by force. She widens her stance and the egg falls from her feet onto the ice, but before he can seize it she has worked it back up onto her feet. Several minutes later she moves her feet apart again, and this time when the egg falls to the ice, the male, still trembling, rolls it between his own feet and up onto them with his beak and "a great deal of difficulty." He and she sing. She stamps around him while he stands "passive and indifferent." They do a mutual display and regard each other's brood patches. She moves away from him, over the ice, but comes back and sings, moves away again but comes back, marches around him, then moves still farther away. He tries to follow her but this time she keeps on going. She'll be away for two months, feeding in the water, while he and the egg stay back on the ice. Already he has been without food for six weeks and he'll be without it for eight or nine more weeks, at the end of which the egg will be hatched, she will have returned from the sea, and it will be his turn to leave, having by then lost up to half his body weight.

Males with eggs aren't the only males on the ice. There are also "unemployed" males. If a male with an egg accidentally drops it, say down a hole in the ice where he can't retrieve it before it freezes, he joins the ranks of the unemployed. Males with eggs are calm and apathetic, but the unemployed are "vivacious," active, and apparently disoriented; they strike out in one direction, then suddenly turn about-face and "look as if they don't know exactly what to do," Prévost wrote. One thing they do know is that they want eggs. At Cape Crozier, Cherry-Garrard saw males, startled by the arrival of humans, abandon their eggs on the ice, and these were "quickly picked up by eggless emperors who had probably been waiting a long time for the opportunity. . . . Such is the struggle for existence" that the poor birds "can only live by a glut of maternity."

So anxious were the males to sit on something, Cherry-Garrard added, "that some of those which had no eggs were sitting on ice! Several times Bill and Birdie [Wilson and Bowers] picked up eggs to find them lumps of ice, rounded and about the right size, dirty and hard." He himself watched as one bird dropped an ice egg, "and again a bird returned and tucked another [ice egg] into itself, immediately forsaking it for a real one, however, when one was offered."

While keeping eggs warm under their belly flaps, males keep themselves warm by "huddling." During particularly bad weather, according to Prévost, hundreds or thousands of males stand tightly pressed together, in a *tortue*, a cluster of birds that apparently looked to some French-speaking person like a turtle's shell (to veteran penguin observer Gerald Kooyman, it looked like a football scrum). A huddle reduces the amount of exposed body surface of each penguin to about a sixth of what it would be if the penguin stood alone. The males stand, backs to the wind, with those on the huddle's windward side peeling off after a while and working their way around until they are on the lee side of the huddle or else in the middle. The huddle thus moves across the ice, as a single body, with a spinning motion, in the direction of the wind.

Almost to the day their chicks hatch, the females return from the sea. After singing and displaying, they pass the contents of their stomachs (fish garnished with crustaceans, Kooyman reports) into the mouths of the chicks. Then they tuck the chicks into their own brood pouches, leaving the males free to go off, at last, to eat. Within weeks, the males come back and pass the contents of *their* stomachs into the chicks' mouths, and the females then head out to sea, and so on. The parents take turns, feeding themselves, feeding their chick.

Should the female be a little late returning at hatching time and the male not able to wait any longer to eat, the maternal glut comes back into play.

"And when at last he simply must go and eat something in the open leads nearby," Cherry-Garrard wrote, "he just puts the child down on the ice, and twenty chickless emperors rush to pick it up. And they fight over it, and so tear it that sometimes it will die. And, if it can, it will crawl into any ice-crack to escape from so much kindness, and there it will freeze."

IT WASN'T UNTIL 1964 that a very large emperor colony was discovered at Cape Washington (by Ian Stirling, the polar bear expert, who was then a Weddell seal expert). One reason it took so long for anyone to find that sizable a colony was that explorers and scientists go to Antarctica in spring and summer, and the colony doesn't exist in those seasons. The evidence of its existence has already gone out with the ice. Penguins that breed on land—and all species except the emperor do—leave broken eggs, guano, dead chicks, and patches of chick down on the ground when they depart. In the emperors' case, the ground melts, and all signs of their having been around vanishes into the sea.

Kooyman, a research professor at the Scripps Institution of Oceanography, arrived at Cape Washington twenty years later, in October (early spring) of 1984. He was dazzled by the sight. Against a backdrop of the Deep Freeze Mountains, there was "a vast stain on the ice," a dark area stretching more than a mile across the horizon, made up of many thousands of penguins. As he watched over the next weeks, he noticed groups forming within the large, amorphous mass of birds, then the groups moving away from each other by several yards a day, "as if the colony were flying apart." By mid-December, groups of chicks formed a semicircle on the ice, with a line of adults running from it all the way to the distant ice edge, from which they departed on their feeding forays. They didn't depart right away, though. The adults milled around on the ice in groups of ten to three hundred birds, restlessly, for hours sometimes. "It's not clear why they hesitate," Kooyman says. He figures they're just trying to assess the safety of the water, decide if predators are waiting for them or not.

Still, there are hungry chicks to feed. "Suddenly, at some unknown signal," Kooyman wrote, "the waiting birds make a single-file dash on their bellies to the edge, driving their feet into the snow like rotary pistons. Watching from the safety of thick ice I was always reminded of a fast-flowing stream tumbling over a waterfall, for in one smooth motion the front birds flop

down to their bellies and toboggan along, while those behind them move up
to the same spot to drop down on their bellies." The penguins gliding along
on their smooth feathers and poling with their feet and flippers reminded
Prévost of skiers.

Emperors don't toboggan on ice, only snow. In more than a decade of
observation, Kooyman has never seen any of them tobogganing on ice. On
ice, they walk. "They have nails very much like crampons," says Kooyman's
son Tory, his assistant one summer. "When walking on bare ice, they dig
their nails in severely." Their feathers and skin hang down so far they don't
have much free leg—"they've got their pants down," Kooyman says—which
makes them less than agile. "They can't run or hop or take high steps."
Their walking pace is slow and measured, "like a coronation march," Kooyman suggests. Going from tobogganing to walking, they use their wings and
beaks to help flip themselves off their bellies and onto their feet. According
to Kooyman, they often use their beaks like a third arm, or an ice pick. To
climb an ice ridge, they may poke their beaks into the ice and pull themselves up.

The chicks leave the Cape Washington colony in mid-December, abruptly,
within ten days of each other. One day Kooyman would see a few chicks on
floes near the edge of the shorefast ice, and three days later he would see hundreds, with lines of chicks leading away from every group on the ice. Some
of the chicks gather on a projecting arm of ice, then more chicks crowd in
behind them, sometimes causing the first chicks to fall in the water. Penguins
do not, however, as is commonly believed, shove one of their number off the
ice edge as a sacrificial victim, to test the water for predators.

With twenty-four thousand chicks a year and a total of seventy-five thousand birds, Cape Washington is clearly a successful colony. Kooyman wondered why. What do penguins want in a colony anyway? Stable ice turned
out to be the key component. In three of the six emperor colonies Kooyman
has studied, the areas of stable ice are small, and they are the ones with the
fewest penguins in them. As the ice under the birds darkens from their
guano and absorbs more sunlight and starts disintegrating, the penguins in
those colonies have no other ice to move to. When he flew over one of the
more successful colonies in the dark of winter and trained a military night-
vision image intensifier on it, he saw seven thousand penguins—"all males,
of course"—standing on the ice, yet to his surprise they were standing "out

in the middle," well away from the rocky windbreak or "any ice ridges or ice falls that could provide shelter." Evidently, being on a stable plate of ice was more important to the birds than getting out of the wind, even in the extreme cold. Deeply impressed by the penguins' grit, Kooyman restated the obvious: "Emperors do a remarkable thing by breeding in the winter."

As for why they breed on ice at all, Kooyman suggests that it may be because huddling, a requirement for males' survival, is best done on a flat surface. Most of the rocky beaches of Antarctica aren't flat, like annual shore-fast ice is. Emperors can go from birth to death without once touching land, the only birds in the world for which that's true. In all the time Kooyman has been studying them, he has never seen a single emperor go ashore, even when it was walking right next to shore. "Ice," Tory says, "is the be-all and end-all of their lives."

Tom Crawford

# The Names of Birds

Getting the names of birds after fifty turns into some
kind of race. You still can't see the finish line—it's not
that bad or good—but you know it's up there. So
when Gary slowed the little pickup outside of
Manchester to point out to me the Greater Scaup
with its stunning blue bill, water bubbling off it as it
pulled up beach kelp, I was surprised and even more
at my immediate feelings of, what can I say, envy,
that he'd got there first, and with so much authority,
the name, the way he already owned it. You couldn't
exactly see the flag he'd planted in that gorgeous
bird's back, but it was there all right. He even
repeated the name, Scaup, for me when I stumbled
trying to say it. Maybe I got even if that doesn't
sound too tit-for-tat when I introduced him to my
humble, little Pied-billed Grebe in its winter plumage
on a walk by Tulalip Bay. I babbled on a bit and being
less than gracious I think I immediately repeated the
name, like I was Shackleton at the South Pole. I don't
know exactly what gets into us after fifty that has us
slowing down at the same time we're speeding up.
Birds pick it up though. We're not coming with a
gun and they know it. That each one has a name and
we're out to learn it, well, that's a human thing
especially if you're our age because there's always
going to be the urgency toward the end and we've
got a lot of birds to go.

J. DREW LANHAM

# Forever Gone

*How bird lives and Black lives intertwine*
*under the long shadow of history*

IMAGINE there is no headstone at the Cincinnati Zoo aviary,
no mark of remembrance, no epitaph. Had there been, it might
have read:

— INCAS —
HERE LIES THE LAST CAROLINA PARAKEET
*CONUROPSIS CAROLINENSIS*
DIED FEBRUARY 21, 1918
HIS LIFE DONE AND BARELY KNOWN,
DOOMED TO THE DARK SWAMP HEREAFTER,
A BIRD FOREVER GONE

Final rites for the passage of one of the most unique birds ever to sweep
across the skies of the American psyche.

There are few creatures that we can tag with exact departure dates, but
with the Carolina parakeet (*Conuropsis carolinensis*), we probably can. It
all ended on February 21, 1918, in the same year World War I came to a
close and not quite four years after the passenger pigeon's own exit from
existence. Incas died that day. He had been housed for some years at the
Cincinnati Zoo aviary and was the last Carolina parakeet anyone would ever
see with certainty.

The passenger pigeon's extinction was sadly predictable. People had
blasted at flocks that once darkened the sky until the birds became scarcer

and scarcer, and then were finally gone. But how the Carolina parakeets' population dwindled down to Incas is a mystery that plagues conservation scientists to this day. It wasn't for lack of the species' range. Despite their name, Carolina parakeets were found across most of the eastern half of the lower forty-eight states. Recent science shows two subspecies—a southeastern population, *Conuropsis carolinensis carolinensis*, that dwelled in the southeast Atlantic, Gulf coastal plains, and all of Florida; and another, *Conuropsis carolinensis ludovicianus*, found west to Texas, Nebraska, and Oklahoma. In some years, birds from the western groups wandered widely and could end up in the Northeast. Wherever they occurred—the North, South, East, or Midwest—mature floodplain bottomland forests lying along great rivers were the parakeets' preferred haunts.

*Conuropsis carolinensis* seemed misplaced in the temperate latitudes. The gaudy tropical combination of its emerald green body, sunset saffron in the wings, and tangerine on the head and cheeks didn't belong here. The Seminole people tagged the bird colorfully: *puzzi la née*, "yellow-headed one." A saberlike tail that would fan to break or bank in a turn, paired with wedge-shaped swept wings, made a pleasing form. Attach a beak hooked and notched like its falcon cousins—but designed in the parrot kind to pry and peel fruits, nuts, and seeds instead of to tear flesh. Its diet varied widely, sycamore and cypress balls among the favorites on the menu, but its affection for one particular seed—cockleburs—was especially noteworthy. An otherwise innocuous weedy plant that grows almost anywhere soil is disturbed, the cocklebur produces thumbnail-size ovate seeds that look like miniature spike-covered footballs. Walk through a tangle of them and you'll soon have the company of hundreds of the needy seeds entangled on your clothes. When it's time to disentangle yourself (and your canine companion) from the unwanted riders, you will need time and patience—the plant's tenacious desire to attach and disperse was an inspiration for hook-and-loop fasteners like Velcro. Beyond being a sticky annoyance and crop pest, cocklebur is highly toxic. Pain and death are the final irritations for many animals that dare to ingest it. Somehow though, Carolina parakeets were immune to the toxic effects and relished the seeds like candy, possibly concentrating the chemicals in their own bodies. Some early naturalists reported cats dying after eating Carolina parakeet entrails.

THREE OWLS

Parrots—a family that includes parakeets, macaws, and cockatoos—are among the prodigies of birds. They have a sense of themselves, of others, and the environment around them that likely extends beyond instinct. Being a parrot means being a thinker who relishes the company of friends and kin—sociality is as much a part of who you are as your plumage. Parrots care. As with us, the long-term parental nurturing and constant preening and feeding exchanges foster a sense of community. That's who parrots are, and who *Conuropsis carolinensis* was—an evolutionarily complex, stunningly beautiful creation whose time was cut short, in part, by individuals not so deeply feeling or thinking.

CHOOSE WILDLIFE conservation as a profession and you're surrounded by loss—marooned on an island of dwindling hopes surrounded by past practices, current lack of care, and emerging policies that can drive the conservationist into psychosis. It can be an unhealthy undertaking that drains one's reserves of hope.

My office walls are covered with portraits of birds gone past existence. At a glance I can see ivory-billed woodpeckers, Bachman's warblers, passenger pigeons, heath hens, great auks, and Labrador ducks. It's an ornithological pantheon of loss. Some Gone Birds, as I call them, especially the ones that would've inhabited my southern home place, have cast spells that I can't shake. As a result, I've carved, collected, and commissioned facsimiles of these birds. I have wooden ivory-bills in abundance and at least a half dozen passenger pigeons scattered around. Even a few Bachman's warblers skulk about. It's a fantastical aviary that serves to sate a desire to un-doom the wondrous loveliness.

Mourning Gone Birds isn't just a dive into a worry hole; it's a dirty crawl into a deep and sandy pit. For each species somehow recovered from oblivion—a bald eagle, for instance—more seem to tumble back in. Whooping cranes, Kirtland's warblers, Gunnison sage-grouse, California condors, and many more teeter on the crater's edge of Almost Gone. Beyond the birds, I mourn the loss of places too, because landscapes degrade and fall into the pit along with the birds. Longleaf pine forests, tallgrass prairies, and salt marshes shrink daily to mere fragments of once expansive swaths. I mourn the Gone Birds and the landscapes they inhabited because the whole of all of us becomes compromised in the loss of some of us.

There are fewer Carolina parakeets in my aviary than any other Gone Bird, though. I have a print or two—and even one life-size figure fashioned from an artfully contrived kaleidoscopic conglomeration of pipe cleaners, a commissioned request from a young friend. That I have fewer parakeets than the other Gone Birds is odd, because for all the birds I've seen alive or dead, mourned and marveled over, all fall behind *Conuropsis carolinensis* in reverence. Thoughts of the extinct bird hang as a gnawing remembering I can't shed, a haint of times past. The idea of a parakeet's flourishes decorating a bald cypress like some sort of feathered ornament grabs me by the heart in a way the others don't. There are no known recordings of the bird's voice and only a few black-and-white photographs of birds kept as pets. Ghosted from existence, it sits now only in memory and museum trays.

Sometimes I seek the validation of what was in natural history museums. Behind what's stuffed and posed for the public facade of museum displays and dioramas are the museums' back rooms and basement catacombs where rows and stacks of dead things lie side by side. Here, the empty-eye socketed souls of creatures killed and collected for science are kept cool and clean to reduce the chances for decay or insect infestation, and are essential tools for the scientist and for conservation.

A few years back, I visited the Georgia Museum of Natural History when there were several Gone Birds on display. It just so happened that at the same time, painter Philip Juras had a number of his relict southern landscapes—portraits of southern river valleys before they were dammed to slowing and scenes of old-growth cypress swamps—hanging around the displays of dead birds. I was drawn into a wormhole that featured the extinct birds, which seemed ready to fly back into the landscapes where they had once lived. There was a feather-worn ivory-billed woodpecker frozen forever in pursuit of a nonexistent grub, and a passenger pigeon perched in loneliness, brainlessly wondering how billions became none. And then there was the Carolina parakeet, which pulled at me with a mesmerizing gravitas. Yes, it was just as dead as the others. There hadn't even been an attempt to pose it on a branch like its peers—it was just a study skin, a tube of feathers meant to be measured and compared to other parakeets.

Something was different about this skin though—it demanded something more than pity for its plight gone past. And then it struck me. I was being watched. Unlike any study skin I'd ever seen of any bird, the cotton-stuffed sack of feathers was watching me. Most stuffed birds have little tufts of cotton protruding from the holes where their eyes used to be, giving them a zombielike appearance. But this particular Carolina parakeet had glossy orbits of yellow glass eyes instead. It lay there unblinking with unsettling eyes that gazed through the display case and through me. Spend time in the company of parrots, and you'll realize quickly (and sometimes uncomfortably) that the birds are thinking on levels beyond asking for crackers. They'll look you over and size you up. Some behaviorists maintain that intelligence in the parrot family can approach that of preschool children—maybe beyond. And although this bird was long past thinking, it appeared thoughtful nonetheless. Maybe it was begging to be released from extinction's damnation, to fly free and play again in the fragments of remaining bald cypress swamps and fallow fields rank with cocklebur.

Studying the parakeet in the museum and surrounded by landscapes that used to be, I began to imagine it among a cohort of others flashing green and gold in small, tight flocks through the used-to-be landscape. In the rendering of an old-growth, south Georgia swamp forest, I could hear the sociable shrieks and jabbering of roosting flocks echoing from the hollow trunks of the buttressed bald cypress. I was expecting the stuffed skin to up and fly away to join a flock wheeling over old fields. Juras's swamps expanded beyond the bounds of the picture frames that held them. Colonnades of gargantuan trees guarded the riverbanks and lorded over expanses of black-water wetland. The parakeets flocked in and out of wilderness that exists now only in ragged remnants of parks and preserves. On the edge of the great swamps we now know by names like Congaree, Great Dismal, Great Black, Okefenokee, Four Holes, and Kissimmee, and all along the South Carolina swamps swollen to flooding by rivers like the Savannah, Edisto, Santee, Combahee, Black, Little and Great Pee Dee, Waccamaw, and Ashepoo, the birds screeched and wheeled in unison. Dodging centuries-old trees and diving in and out of shafts of morning sunlight, they squawked their way to where the deep forest ended and yielded to open lands and farms.

I found myself completely consumed in my imagination: suddenly, I can see the flock circling once, twice, and then on the third pass settling into an old field gone fallow. The unplanted plot is a weedy unkempt affair choked with ragweed and cockleburs. The burry bane of many a farmer's existence, the weeds are beginning to throw their sticky seed to whatever furred thing might pass by and offer a ride to the next patch of soil. To the parakeets though, the burrs aren't pests—they're a delicacy. With great screeching in a celebration of food finding, the parakeets land and settle into a squabbling feast. They hang and dangle like green and gold chickadees from waist-high weeds. Tender bits from the tough burrs are consumed, and the rough, sterile husks dropped to the ground. But then suddenly, the whole flock is up in the sky again in a panicked, shrieking flurry—a watchful companion warning of a raptor overhead. The swallow-tailed kite wheeling below the clouds says *danger* in the moment. And then, just as suddenly, a calm falls over them—a rapid understanding of the lack of threat from the graceful raptor whose eating interests focus on dragonflies. The flock settles again in garrulous gathering to resume the meal. They are mostly welcomed there as they digest the undesirable weed in a form of service that the farmers—and the enslaved people working in the fields—appreciate. The more burrs the parakeets destroy, the less prep to do to the field for growing crops again. Like my grandmother, Mamatha, used to say: many hands make light work. It is a scene many across the range of the species likely witnessed.

John James Audubon captured the essential character of *Conuropsis carolinensis*, painting them gleefully entangled in a thicket of cocklebur. In one of his most popular works, the birds seem consumed with consuming but acutely aware, too, of the world around them. They're engaged with their food; engaged with one another; engaged with us almost two hundred years beyond the painting. Facing the portrait, you count a flock of seven. A female on the far left raises a foot. Maybe Audubon meant to show the bird in mid-scratch or stretching to reach for the next cocklebur. Because art is also about what the seer sees, I imagine her waving at whomever might be looking from beyond the frozen frame of an existence that was already waning in Audubon's time. To me, it has always seemed an invitation to come closer—one knowing being to another.

ALTHOUGH AMERICA was burgeoning at its seams when Carolina parakeets flew about in abundance, it was a nation still wildly rough around the edges. What remained in the hinterlands is what eco-restorationists sometimes refer to as *baseline*—a reference condition for return.

As an ecologist of color, I find the restorative thinking a bittersweet exercise. I've been steeped in the training (or brainwashing) of the "bring-back-the-natives-undam-the-rivers-pull-up-the-privet-and-release-the-bison" paradigm. It's a wistful conjuring to make North America great again—in an ecologically good way, I suppose. But beyond the uncomfortable verbiage about casting out exotics and eliminating aliens, there is the question of who—beyond the largely homogenous choir of restoration ecologists and wistful wishers for the good old days of yore—gets to say what wild nature is. There has been a slow admission of Indigenous American contribution to the landscape, and the ways in which they managed the land that sustained their communities and culture. For ecologists, it means recognizing the role that people of color—who preceded ecologists and their almost exclusively white conservation "movement"—played in shaping nature, and what those people knew about the North American landscape before they did.

Wishing for a contrived, humanless wildness forwards a practice of belittling—or ignoring altogether—"colored" land connection. My own dark-hued roots are mired in the soil of the American South. When I drive by, fly over, or walk through most places "down here," I can see and often feel the actions of my ancestors who changed the land. By connecting the pain of that past to what we see now, I pay homage and deepen my personal connection with place. Yes, it's an exorcism of past pain, but also a progression toward helping others see the land's real history, and perhaps to become reconnected with the land. My desire to inform and inspire, beyond mere ecology, grows daily. Along with the fate of the Gone Birds and their lost worlds, it possesses me.

I wonder about the enslaved watchers who worked in the shadows of endless passenger pigeon flocks that passed overhead, or heard the ivory-bills that called from the tall timber, or glanced the Carolina parakeets that flashed across work-weary eyes. I think about salt marshes modified and maintained by enslaved Senegalese—the spring crop waving thick with Carolina Gold rice and Sea Island cotton that created some of the richest men in the world. Beyond the monotonous thud slice of a hoe in pluff mud, what would my ancestors have noticed? The day-to-day work of survival required more than brawn and will. From where would hope emerge? Humans have always looked skyward for inspiration, imagining themselves unbound by gravity or the weight of oppression. Flight means freedom. It is not beyond the oppressed to lean hard on natural beauty as an uplifting beam. Survival draws on inspiration. Sweet sounds and beauty are no less worthy of notice because one is in chains—perhaps they are worthier because of the chains.

For the enslaved, they would have noticed more about the parakeets than just their beauty. The parakeets lived in tight-knit social groups composed of relatives. Along with crows and jays, the parakeets would have been the avian intellectuals in a landscape where they had to make do with not only what was, but also with what was to come. And then they were servants, too, clearing fields of cocklebur and sandspur menace. But when the birds exercised a desire to have more—to eat the fruit from plantation and farm orchards—the parakeets became targets of persecution. Because of their social nature, birds not killed or wounded in the first round of extermination circled around their fallen family members that screamed in fear and injury. In that empathy, more birds fell.

I imagine the flock, assaulted and driven out of a ripening orchard of plums and pears. On the edge of day, as katydids call in dusk, the birds retreat to the forests to roost in cavernous hollows. A depleted flock reenters a shrinking swamp domain—remnants of wild southern places already disappearing along with the parakeets. They are home, finding comfort in the shadows of last light. But daily, it seems, in smaller and smaller numbers and in fewer and fewer acres.

The birds aren't alone in the refuge. There are humans in the shadows, too. Torches lit from knots of fatwood throw long shadows onto the hollow trunks where the parakeets roost. The dark forms are Maroons, self-liberated slaves who once worked the same plantations that the parakeets frequent. They were once chattel, bound to the land at the cruel behest of white planters, but who escaped terror and freed themselves from the very fields over which the birds have flown and fed. As the Carolina parakeets find security in wooded wetlands, so too do the Maroons—slave chasers and the "law" hesitate to pursue them into the swamps. Free from the plight of overseers and forced labor, they lived for decades in thriving communities within mere miles of the plantations they fled.

The Maroons shared the Carolina parakeets' requisite for freedom. They found sustenance in the wilderness, but also made nocturnal forays back onto the plantations to secure food, tools, and sometimes weapons. They traced the same paths as the parakeets, but worked the night shift. It was a life on the edge with constant threats of persecution, capture, and death. But it was a free life and that matters most. The land was flush with grain and fruit that only existed because of Black hands. What Maroons took was just reclamation for work done.

By the time Audubon noted the Carolina parakeet's decline in the 1830s, the enslavement economy, fueled by whip-cracked backs, had pushed the country toward a sinful prosperity. It wasn't just the South that benefited. North of the Mason-Dixon line, wealth flowed upstream to financial houses and investors. The numbers of Black people in bondage exploded, and as enslavement swelled, the numbers of *Conuropsis carolinensis* dwindled. And within little more than a generation of Audubon's lamentation that "our Parakeets are very rapidly diminishing in number," a civil war was raging across much of the birds' range.

Persecution of any kind ultimately demands relief, whether through escape or revolt. It's all an inalienable flight to self-determination. It's a risky thing to seek one's own destiny, though. The decision to leave certain bad for uncertain good is the balance that must be measured. Enslaved people knew the gamble, and some decided that liberty had to be sought at any cost, whatever consequences might come. And so when the Maroons fled to the southern swamps and found something way better than being held captive, they shared the refuge with other beings that ultimately found refuge there, too. In the convergence of demands for human dignity and freedom, and nonhuman survival and existence, islands of empathy emerge between our braided-river beings.

Human trade and trafficking, genocide, driving other creatures to extinction—all are built on a corrupt human belief that some are worthier than others. Racism and white supremacy lie at the heart of enslavement—you could be bought and sold, whipped, raped, or killed on a whim. It was custom, practice, and policy, and the basis of so much of the brutality and bias we experience today. It begins with the belief that some are superior and some are inferior—both racism and sending another species into the oblivion of extinction grow from the same rotten core.

THE PARAKEETS' big-timbered bottomland world shrank even more rapidly after the Civil War and disappeared altogether into the ramped-up hyper-greed of early twentieth-century land grabs, rampant timbering, and swamp-busting agriculture. The fast-dwindling populations of Carolina parakeets

GET THAT BUG

were assaulted on several sides, sending the species plummeting. Beyond habitat loss, other factors probably contributed to the decline, including competition with introduced European honeybees for tree cavities; demands for bright feathers for women's hats; and persecution as pests. Although the birds cleared fields of cockleburs, crop depredation was likely an incentive for killing *Conuropsis carolinensis*. A flock descending on a ripening orchard or cornfield undoubtedly cost the species dearly, and the strong social ties that caused individual birds to flock around the fallen was a fatal compounding factor. As agriculture spread across the landscape, so did new diseases. Some scientists postulate that the parakeet's exposure to poultry diseases may have been a final nail in the forever-gone coffin.

And then there was the irony of rarity. As reports of declines spread among the ornithological community, both professionals and amateurs "needed" to add birds and eggs to their collections. Collectors—many of them obsessed hoarders—shot whole flocks for the sake of "science." The museum bird that wouldn't release me from its gaze likely fell in the name of "knowledge" and the need to possess a rare thing with no thought of its extinction.

Today, when I lead others out to bird-watch in the remaining fragments of wild places, I cannot help but bring the history of the enslaved, and the landscape we tread upon, into the same head-heart space. I cannot tell stories of birds and of the cypress swamps and old rice fields I frequent in Lowcountry South Carolina without telling the story of those who moved forests, soil, and water through force and greed. Stories in the soil have to be plowed up.

Hate, enslavement, persecution, and the dramatic changes to the land wrought by all of us are heavy burdens to bear. Maybe it's why I yet seek birds, here and gone on. The quest renders the remaining feathered things precious gifts, passed forward to survive it all. Black ducks and black rails in "managed" rice impoundments are reminders of what was created by a cruel society on the backs of Black people. We can't separate one from the other. Can efforts to steward and make conservation a more inclusive effort be bolstered now by informing others of the past connections, even when they are painful recollections? Telling the full story seems the best start. Signs and monuments must tell the whole story—including the human elements—painful as it may be, behind the present things we see. Black land ownership and connections to nature languish in many places where Carolina parakeets may have once brightened the skies. History's shadow can be a long one, especially when cast cruelly or when remedies to right wrongs are made without consideration for everyone and everything. Do we readily reveal these chapters in history? Does conservation bear a responsibility to illuminate the dark corners where not only birds and beasts have suffered, but humans have as well? If Aldo Leopold's admonition to keep every "cog and wheel" is the first step in tinkering with the ecology, then the cultural gears and switches certainly warrant our consideration.

For those birds gone on, I mourn. I mourn the Carolina parakeets persecuted as pests and shot down for simply being who they were. Their plumage and behavior became easy marks to profile and possess for selfish purposes. I think of Incas, imprisoned as his species was on the brink of extinction, no crime committed other than being what he was. I see parallels between the Gone Birds and who I am as a Black American man. The mistreatment of nature, the disrespect for all those things believed unworthy of enough respect to not drive them into the pit of never-ness, has common plight among people who've been slighted by practice, privilege, and policy. Extinction by human hands is a sin. Racism is no different. It is a callousness built on judgmental whim. We are all part and parcel of nature, parakeets and people alike. How we treat one another determines who we all are—or might become. The good of it, our attempts to do better by birds and other species as well as each other, spells hope on one side. The upwelling of ignorance and denial of what's been, what is, and what could be, and a blind march headlong into some unregulated regained greatness with the past as the meter to follow spells certain doom. It is an evil directed at birds and humans, too. It is a callousness toward life that spells endangerment, extinction, and exclusion.

In my constant quest for birds, thinking of those gone and then reveling in the ones still with us, I also find a peace and momentary freedom from the bad that exists in the world. In my escapes to places where birdsong drowns out the news stream and a soaring swallow-tailed kite blinds me to all else except the innate desire to fly in self-determination and free will, the bad disappears for a while and I too am marooned. I become a Maroon—escaping certain bonds to find freedom in the deep recesses of wildness.

MORE THAN A HUNDRED YEARS since Incas died. In the years of wishful sightings since—a disputed sighting on the South Carolina Santee Delta, ghosts in the Georgia Okefenokee, shadows flying across the Florida Okeechobee prairie—other species have fallen silent. Most have faded with no epitaph to mark their place in the Gone Birds book. For all the reasons posited for their loss, it usually comes down to a lack of caring. And more than that—pushing a living being into the abyss of extinction is, in the end, a hate crime, a lack of compassion for another's implicit right to exist. I feel some kinship in that place, where my being is seen by some as worthless.

Those responsible for Incas's well-being had to know the species' rare status as they watched his last moments. What kind of relationship did he have with those keepers in the Cincinnati Zoo? Did Incas respond to their voices in parrot squawks and chortles, or maybe knowing parrot nods of his big-beaked head? What were those last moments like? Was there a rift in the cosmos, or a ripple somewhere "out there"? For a species whose disappearance lies in so many ill lots, many believed that those final days of the last Carolina parakeet ultimately came down to a broken heart. His mate, Lady Jane, had died a few months before, and Incas was reported to be lonely.

More than a century later and there's talk of "reversing" the crime. Parakeet fanciers discuss resequencing genes from dead birds in museum trays to reassemble a Frankenstein-esque *Conuropsis carolinensis*. For me, the de-extinction discussion is a hollow one. How does an organism adapt to the missing gaps in time when it didn't exist? How does a species absent for a century react to a landscape so dramatically altered as to present a different planet than the one it knew? Technology tells us it may not be an impossible task, but maybe such tasks should be ones we let pass. The whole of what a Carolina parakeet, or passenger pigeon, or Bachman's warbler was will always be more than the engineered sum of its parts. In the century since Incas's eyes dimmed, we should have let what we've done to make living things gone stand as monuments, so as to not let that history repeat itself.

At the time of Incas's death, there was no policy demanding notice or care for Carolina parakeets as an "endangered species"—such policies wouldn't exist for another fifty-five years. Maybe it wouldn't have mattered. And although policy and regulation are part of what we need to prevent tragedies like what happened to the parakeet, maybe something simpler is needed just as badly. If we see ourselves bound together in all of it—humans and nonhumans alike—then maybe care takes on a deeper meaning. We all require the same clean air and water, safe places to land, roost, and love whomever we choose. Treat others, regardless of plumage or color of skin, the way you long to be treated.

EVEN STILL, as I sat in my office, surrounded by my facsimiles and replicas of the Gone Birds, the parakeet left me longing for something I can't quite explain. I wanted, in my own way, to see the bird live again, to feel its animated, flying, screeching, and squawking for myself. There's a bit of a god complex in most ecologists. Most of us aren't just watchers and data miners; we're also wannabe creators.

And so I created my own parakeet, tacked and fastened together with wood glue and wanting. I worked for weeks researching the bird, trying to get a handle on the sense of it, its emergent being. After days of measuring, cutting, discarding, remeasuring, and recutting, I spent more days fitting and refitting the pieces together as if I could bring *Conuropsis carolinensis* back again. The wings at first were too wide—not fast enough to carry the bird quickly through the past. I narrowed them and posed them downward. How to pose the tail in profile? I first splayed it out, but then decided I wanted it straight as an arrow, so there'd be no delays in its travel. The bird's face needed to be parrotesque accurate, parrot precise. I scroll-cut an eternal scream in the hawk-hooked beak, could almost hear a muffled squawk. I layered on thin coats of painted plumage, then wiped them away to add another. Finally, after a fortnight of fussing, a last coat of subtle shading, and a little wish conjuring, I set two bulging, brown taxidermy eyes in place, and shuddered a bit inside as something gone forever stared back. A Gone Bird lay in my hand ready to fly—and it seemed to be asking me why. I placed him among the rafters of my writing shack, where he now spins in the slightest breeze, bound for someplace far beyond my seeing.

W. TODD KANEKO

# Naming the Birds

The beach is noiseless,
stretching behind my father's house,
a mile of stones and driftwood

for those herons, ghostlike,
carefully picking their way
down the shoreline,

all knees and neck,
looking for crabs or something
they lost in the surf, and my father

points at them and says their names
like he is making a wish.
Then they are all gone and it's just me

and the seagulls hover overhead
saying their own names,
the sky making those sounds

airplanes make when the world
has nothing left to say to you.

I have no memory of any wish
of mine coming true, no knowledge
of how a man turns to another man
and promises never to leave him,

but the other day I named the shadow
of a cardinal through a frosty window

for my son, described it so he would
know it when he sees one for himself.

TRANSFORMATION

FRED MARCHANT

# Thereinafter

crested
and hungry
but nowhere seen
only
the sound
of its pecking
hollow
branch offered
the yielding bronze
bell
of memory
the log striker
words
welling up
with unbidden laughter

JOHN T. PRICE

# Man Killed by Pheasant

S
o I'M DRIVING east on Highway 30 toward Cedar Rapids, Iowa. It's a four-lane and because I'm an eldest child, I'm driving the speed limit, around fifty-five, sixty miles per hour. I'm listening to Hendrix cry "Mary"—imagining, as usual, that I am Hendrix— when in the far distance I see some brown blobs hovering across the highway: one, then two. By the way they move, low and slow, I guess they're young pheasants. But two is a pretty small brood, I think, so as I near the place of their crossing I look to the right, across the empty passenger seat and into the grassy ditch to see if I can spot the whole clan. Suddenly there is a peripheral darkness, like the fast shadow of an eclipse, and something explodes against the side of my head, erupting into a fury of flapping and scratching and squawking. Somehow, in an act of almost miraculous timing, one of the straggling pheasants has flown in my driver's side window. And being the steel-jawed action hero I am, I scream, scream like a rabbit, and strike at it frantically with my left arm, the car swerving, wings snapping, Hendrix wailing, feathers beating at my face until, at last, I knock the thing back out the window and onto the road. I regain control of the car, if not myself, and pull over, to cry.

That's the time I should have been killed by a pheasant. For a couple of reasons peculiar to that summer, I recall it often. It occurred, for one, while I was on my way to teach a technical writing course at a nearby community college. This "distance learning experience" took place exclusively by radio wave, with me in an empty room on campus and my fifteen students scattered at sites within a hundred-mile radius. The technology was such that my students could see me, but I couldn't see them. To converse we had to push buttons at the base of our microphones, so that each class felt like an episode of *Larry King Live*: *Judy from Monticello, hello, you're on the air.* "The future of higher education," my supervisor called it. And I never did get the hang of the camera. I'd turn it on at the beginning of the class and there, on the big-screen monitor in front of me, would be a super close-up of my lips. I'd spend the next few minutes jostling the joystick, zooming in and out like one of those early music videos until I found the suitable frame. Sometimes my students would laugh at this, and I'd hear them laughing, but only if they pushed their buttons. If there was an electrical storm nearby, I wouldn't hear them laugh at all.

On the way to such a displaced, bodiless job, a near-death experience had some additional currency. As did the larger natural disaster unfolding around me. It was the summer of the great Iowa floods, 1993, and the reason I was on Highway 30 to begin with was that my usual route to campus had been washed out by the swollen Iowa River. This was a serious situation—people had been killed, and Des Moines, our distant capital, had been without water for more than a week. "Nature Gone Mad!" the national news media called it.

Although aware of the widespread suffering, I was privileged to watch the whole thing unfold more gently from the roadways of my rural commutes. And what I saw was a wilderness of birds. Bean fields suddenly became sheer, inaccessible places where egrets stood piercing frogs in the shallows, where pelicans flew in great cyclonic towers, where bald eagles swung low to pick off stranded fish. Perched on soggy, neglected fence posts were birds I hadn't seen since early childhood, bobolinks and bluebirds and tanagers. Their color and song drew my eye closer to the earth, to the ragged ditches full of forgotten wildflowers and grasses—primrose and horsemint, big blue and switch—safe, at least for a while, from the mower's blade. The domesticated landscape of my home had gone wild and I was mesmerized by it.

Toward the end of the summer flooding, when the dramatic presence of wild birds dwindled, I thought a lot about Noah, about those end days on the ark between the release of the raven and the return of the dove, between a knowledge of a decimated landscape and a faith in one that, through decimation, had become reborn. I wondered if Noah, like me, was of mixed emotions, suspended between hope and despair, witnessing the floodwaters swell then recede, the wetlands become crop fields again, the wilderness become tame, the unknown become known, the miraculous become mundane.

When it was all over, I thought I understood Noah's first impulse, once on dry land, to get drunk and forget. I had lived my entire life in Iowa, the most ecologically devastated state in the Union, with less than one-tenth of one percent of its native prairie habitats remaining. "Tragic" is what the ecologist Wes Jackson has called the plowing up of this prairie region; "one of the two or three worst atrocities committed by Americans." Not that I'd ever cared—it's hard to care about a wild place you've never seen or known. Yet in those short, flooded months of 1993, I witnessed a blurry reflection of what Iowa had once been: a rich ecology of wetlands and savannas and prairies, alive with movement and migration. Alive with power. Under its influence, I felt closer to my home landscape than ever before. So when that power slipped from view, I was surprised to find myself in grief, longing to chase after it. But where would I look? Having spent most of my life wanting to leave the Midwest, in what place or experience might I find the reasons to stay, to commit?

Death by pheasant didn't immediately come to mind. Although, in the wake of the floods, death was part of what I longed for. Or rather the possibility of a certain kind of death, one that, appropriately enough, is associated with birds. You know the kind of death I'm talking about, to become lost in a vast landscape, to die, as Edward Abbey has described it, "alone, on rock under sun at the brink of the unknown, like a wolf, like a great bird. . . ." It is the kind of potential death that in my mind helps define wilderness as a place worthy of respect, a place of consequence and power and a kind of fearful freedom. My German friend calls this freedom *vogelfrei*, which loosely translates into "free as a bird." Far from the positive gist we associate with this phrase, vogelfrei refers to the state of being cast out from the tribe, so free you will die in the open, unburied, to be picked apart by birds. It is a state of fear and vulnerability and movement, one that might have the ability, especially here in the agricultural Midwest—a place seemingly without fang, without claw, without talon—to make us more observant of the natural world, more humbled by its power to transform us.

At first flush, my collision with the pheasant didn't seem to hold that kind of possibility. But it could have. If, for example, this had happened to me as a child or adolescent or as a member of a New Age men's group, I might have made something more of it. After all, as a boy some of my favorite comic book heroes were mutations of man and animal—Spider-Man, for example, and Dr. Lizard, and Captain America's sidekick, the Falcon. Imagine, in my case, the comic book story that could have developed: a mild-mannered English professor is struck in the head by a wayward pheasant, his blood mingling with the bird's while, coincidentally, a cosmic tsunami from a distant stellar explosion soaks the whole scene in gamma radiation. Emerging from the smoldering rubble: Pheasant Man. No, *Super* Pheasant Man! As Super Pheasant Man, our mild-mannered professor finds he has acquired some of the bird's more powerful features—its pride and daring, its resilience, its colorful head feathers—learning to use them for the good of humanity while at the same time fighting the darker side of his condition, namely, a propensity for polygamy and loose stools.

But I was not a boy when I met that unlucky pheasant on Highway 30, which is too bad, because for a long time afterward I found nothing particularly hopeful or uplifting or powerful about the experience. Instead, I saw my life, and death, made a joke, just like the place where I grew up. Imagine the regional headlines: *Iowa Man Killed by Pheasant. Mother Files for Hunting License.* Imagine the funeral where, in the middle of singing "I'll Fly Away," one of my more successful cousins whispers to his wife: *And it wasn't even a big cock pheasant that killed him. It was just a little baby pheasant.* And imagine that hypothetical men's group who, in their wailful mourning of my death, botch up the spirit animal ritual and condemn my soul to be borne not on the wings of an eagle or a falcon, but on those of a pheasant, stubby and insufficient, struggling to get us both off the ground, never getting more than maybe fifteen feet toward heaven before dropping back down to earth with a thud and a cluck.

No thank you. I do not wish to become one with the pheasant, either in this life or in the next. Yet I wonder if there isn't something to our togetherness. Seen through the history of the land, this bird and I have been colliding for centuries. Having evolved together on the grasslands of distant continents, we were both brought to this country by the accidents of nature and technology and voyage. As Americans, the pheasant and I have come to share cultural ties to certain important historical figures, like Benjamin Franklin, whose son-in-law was one of the first to attempt to introduce the ring-necked pheasant, a native of China, to this country. (His release was unsuccessful, partly, I'd like to think, because it occurred in New Jersey.) Its introduction to Iowa more than a century later was also by accident, taking place during a 1901 windstorm near Cedar Falls that blew down confinement fences and released two thousand of the birds into the prairie night. They've remained here ever since, sharing with my people an affinity for the northern plains to which we've both become anchored by the peculiarities of the soil. This soil, loess, and glacial till, migrant and invasive, like us, having been carried here from ancient Canada by wind and by ice. Its rich organic loam, black as oil, brought my farmer ancestors to the region and has, at the same time, held close the range of the ring-necked pheasant, lacing the bird's grit with calcium carbonate. Because the ringneck requires an abundance of this mineral, it doesn't stray far, not even a few hundred miles south into the gray prairies of, say, lower Illinois. Although the soil there is slightly older, shaved from native limestone, it is, for the pheasant, less nutritious.

So, the pheasant and I remain settlers in this region, watching as others of our kind move on or migrate. As such, we have come to share some of the same enemies, like the fencerow-to-fencerow, get-big-or-get-out agricultural policies of the 1970s and '80s. These policies, enacting yet another vision of migration, dramatically expanded agricultural exports and, at the same time, led the region to the farm crisis of the 1980s, to the flight and impoverishment and, sometimes, death of thousands of industrial and farm families. For the pheasant as well, despite set-aside programs, this fencerow-to-fencerow world has held its own kind of impoverishment, a destruction of habitat so thorough that two hundred pheasants have been known to crowd a shelterbelt only a hundred yards long. In such a bare-naked world a good blizzard, like the one in 1975, has the power to wipe out 70 to 80 percent of a local pheasant population in a single evening.

Yet in sharing enemies, we have also been, together, the common enemy. To the prairie chicken, for instance—one of the many native citizens that had the unfortunate luck to precede us here in the "heartland." For almost a century European settlers hunted and plowed down prairie chicken populations in Iowa. But some argue it was the ring-necked pheasant that finished it off, destroying its eggs, occupying its nests, and interrupting, seemingly out of spite, its dancing-ground rituals. Since then, efforts to restore prairie chickens have usually had to correspond with significant reductions in pheasant populations. Most of those efforts have failed, largely because reducing pheasant numbers around here is about as easy and popular as reducing our own. The difficulties are partly economic: In Iowa, we hunt and eat this bird to the tune of about 300,000 a year. It's one of our biggest tourist attractions. But I wonder, too, if we don't see in this bird, at some unconscious level, a dark reflection of our own troubling history in the American grasslands, our role as ecological party crashers, as culture wreckers. Our role, ultimately, as killers and thieves. To question the pheasant's claim on the land is, in some way, to question our own.

It's unfair, of course, and dangerous to project our sins onto another species. When tossing around ethical responsibility, the difference between us, between instinct and intent, is significant. But the pheasant needn't worry about taking the blame. Hardly anyone around here gives them a second thought. That indifference was part of my problem when searching for reasons to care about my home landscape. In relation to that bird, as to most of the familiar, transplanted wildlife around me, I felt nothing. The pheasant was common, and the last thing I wanted to feel as a midwesterner was common. Since early adolescence I'd been fleeing a sense of inadequacy shared by many in this region, a sense of self marked—as Minnesotan Patricia Hampl has said—by "an indelible brand of innocence, which is to be marked by an absence, a vacancy. By nothing at all." For midwesterners like me, the complex, the worthy seemed always to be found elsewhere. Not here in this ordinary place, this ordinary life.

So not surprisingly, during the years following the floods, I sought a new relationship to the Midwest not in the ragged and familiar land immediately around me, but in the distant and, in my imagination, more exotic landscapes of the Black Hills and Badlands in western South Dakota. What I discovered in those places did indeed transform me. I saw for the first time elk bugling and mating, at home on their native prairies. While sitting in a fly-plagued prairie dog town, I saw for the first time a bison bull wallowing in the brown dust. On the grasslands near Bear Butte, where Crazy Horse once sought vision, I saw for the first time a falcon stoop to kill a mallard, the native cycles of predator and prey, of wild death, still lingering. Even vogelfrei, that fearful freedom—I felt it for the first time in this region while walking lost in the deep earth of the Badlands. My journey through these distant places toward commitment has been awkward, fragmented, and at times pathetic, even comic. Yet the significance of these experiences cannot be underestimated, how they have worked to cure a lifetime of ignorance and indifference. How, to use spiritual terms, they have filled what once was empty.

But if the spiritual journey to a place begins, as Kathleen Norris claims, with fear, then it was not the bison or the falcon or the Badlands that first drew me closer to the region in which I had been raised. It was the pheasant. That particular baby pheasant—there on a highway in eastern Iowa—which almost, as my sister would say, rocked my world. In a sense, that's exactly what it did. It made me wake up, become more observant of what's lurking in the margins. What's lurking there, despite the rumors, is the possibility of surprise, of accident, of death. And if it's possible in this overdetermined landscape for a pheasant to kill a man, then why not, too, the possibility of restoration, renewal, and, at last, hope?

But that's a romantic stretch, and at the time of the incident itself I didn't feel particularly worshipful of its surprise. As I sat in the car wiping hot tears from my face, I just felt lucky—*thank God it wasn't a two-lane!*—and then ridiculous. The whole thing was so absurd it might have been a dream. I carefully leaned my head out the window to see if the pheasant was still on the road. It wasn't. I thought about going back to find it, to see if it was injured, but decided against it—after all, it was only a pheasant. Besides, I was late for work where in a few minutes I would be taking my own precarious flight through the airwaves, across the flooded land, to students I would never see, never truly know.

I started the car and eased back onto the highway. As I approached cruising speed, I saw something move out of the corner of my eye. I jerked, swerving the car a little. A feather. An ordinary brown feather. Then another and another—there must have been a dozen of them—floating in the breeze of the open window. They tickled and annoyed me. Yet for reasons I still can't explain, I kept the window open—just a crack—enough to keep the feathers dancing about the cabin. And that's how I, the man almost killed by a pheasant, drove the rest of those miles, touched by its feathers in flight, touched by an intimacy as rare and welcome, in my tragic country, as laughter in a storm.

WHITE BIRD DANCE

BLAS FALCONER

# The Hummingbird

A blur in the periphery,
like the mind if the mind

were airborne, a buzz among
leaf and orange blossom,

the long beak pressing quick
into flower after flower, high

on each sweet center, and
each iridescent feather shines

hard—a thought, half-formed,
charged, a hum before it lights

on the branch—and you
see it clearly—dimmed, now,

small, no longer what it was.

Deb Olin Unferth

# Chicken
# Disenthralled

HEN, ALONE, strolling away from the eight looming apparatuses of Happy Green Family Farm. Her first steps on dirt, not wire.

Most industry hens out of a cage for the first time would never walk off into a chilly day after a life spent in a cage. Most would be crowded up against a wall under an overhang or hiding in a bush, trying to get back inside so as not to be prey to whatever the hell was up there: sky and all its certain evils. Bred to cower, you might say. But here was this enterprising (imprudent?) hen, Bwwaauk, as she was known to herself.

How had Bwwaauk gotten herself into this predicament?

HERE THEY ARE, barricaded in their concrete barns. They're dug in, ready—though they don't know what or who is coming. They wait behind ramparts of drying excrement, behind fans six feet high. The farm people, the few left on the prairie, the holdout humans.

Here's the barn manager. The truckers, the mechanics. The pop and depop crew. These are the desk people, a few to a farm. These are the families.

The land. Its grand width, long horizon, its coordinates, its unmarked roads that cut through hand-size towns and run flat and straight.

These are the barns. They're made up of belts and birds and catwalks, ten lux of illumination and the eight-degree slope of a hen's floor. From airplanes they look like lined-up sticks of gum. Thousands of tons of feed, hundreds of acres of steel bent again and again into a labyrinth of right angles. Guests are asked to step into disinfectant footbaths before coming in, like a liquid welcome mat.

Here are the manuals, the animal movement logs, the light programs, the beak-trimming protocol. The amount of carbon dioxide gas used for mass extermination. These are the farmers. An endangered species, each year a handful fewer than the year before, as the farmlands slowly depopulate (and the number of eggs grows and grows). Men built like blocks atop very clean, very white tennis shoes. They wear plain wedding bands, jeans pulled up to here. Republicans, old-style white men, Christians. An ultrapolite command, they exude a controlled calm. They can be glimpsed leaving the conference room, pausing at reception.

None of these people went into farming because they hate chickens, for Christ's sake. What do you think? It's the eggs, the eggs, so many being made that if they didn't come to work, who knows what would happen? We used to eat eggs a few times a year, but now they are everywhere, emerging from the nation's farms at an alarming rate, 110 billion a year. Citizens must eat as many as we can. It is our patriotic duty. We must put them into all of our meals, all of our batters and breads and spreads and sauces, our breakfasts, on top of our meat or under it, inside our sandwiches, into all our snacks one way or another, our power bars and chocolate. But still that won't be enough. Still more eggs are coming, piling up on the belts, leaving the farms, assembling on the grocery shelves, into refrigerators, more and more and more. We must soldier on, find other ways to consume them. We must put them on our faces, in our hair. We could grind up the shells and make toothpaste. We could build rocket ships and shoot the yolks off into space, small suns; we could explode them and smear them across a daylight sky.

Bwwaauk had spent her life from the time she was a pullet on this farm.

You'd think that by now with all the genetic meddling, sensory deprivation, and inbreeding, 150 years' worth, that these animals would barely have brains anymore, that their minds' dials would be set on static, a low hum, refrigeration vibration. You'd think they'd be blank-brained, a collection of impulses and flesh. Indeed, some of the hens on Happy Green Family Farm were moronic slabs, but most were not. They all contained within them the DNA, if not the full expression, of the original bird intelligence. Those hardy genes pressed themselves into existence in all kinds of ways, so that most of these hens still had that feral smart-bird spark in the eye, the instinctual *Gallus* need to flock, wander, arrange themselves into hierarchies, mate, rear, befriend, follow, fly their awkward short flights, bathe and preen in the dust.

Those hundreds of thousands of brains of Happy Green Family Farm were ticking away in those grim warehouses, crushed into tiny boxes (or crowded into larger boxes in the two so-called cage-free barns), half-smothered and rotting alive in the oppressive air, barely able to spread their wings, unable to look up and see anything but steel and conveyor belts and low-wattage bulbs, pressed up against strangers, beaks half-severed, feet deformed by the wire they stood on day and night.

Bwwaauk had grown up in Barn 8, an old-style A-frame structure, where the cages are piled in tiers on a slant so that when the shit drops through the wire, it misses (mostly) the hens in the lower tiers. Bwwaauk had lived in a bottom-row cage, the worst spot on an A-frame because shit drops on you from above (the system isn't perfect). The whole jalopy is placed on the second floor of the barn with a large opening underneath. The excrement falls through the wire to a huge open room below called the pit.

Barn 8 was the oldest barn on the farm, built in 1990. Its cages were rusty. In places the wire had corroded and had holes in it, holes the size of a chicken. In most rows, if a hole broke through the rust and a hen fell through, she simply landed in the cage below her. The hens in that cage would peck her to death as an invader, then stand on her dead or dying body to give their feet a rest from the wire. But in Bwwaauk's case, when the ammonia ate through the rust and broke open her cage on the bottom row, she flopped down onto a six-foot pile of excrement.

She landed with a thump. She looked up at the cage she'd just left. The hens in the cage peered down through the hole at her below. They all assessed the situation.

IN THE WILD, chickens have complicated cliques and distinct voices. They talk among themselves, even before they hatch. A hen twitters and sings to her eggs, and the chicks inside answer, peeping and burbling and clicking through the shells. Adult chickens have more than thirty categories of conversation, each with its own web of coos and calls and clucks and struts.

Chickens gossip, summon, play, flirt, teach, warn, mourn, fight, praise, and promise.

It is this last, *promise*, that concerns us here.

In a cage situation a hen has little use for most of these categories of conversation. Her vocabulary atrophies or never fully develops—but it's there, contained within the brain (which stores and processes information differently from the human brain—the bird's brain is more like a microchip folded inside the cortex, not like the human's bulky car motor) and will surface when necessary.

So it was that in the moment Bwwaauk turned her face up to the hens in the cage she'd just fallen from, she struggled to communicate, her mind turned on. Winked to life.

There is a particular cheep isolated by bird researchers who specialize in the *Gallus gallus*. This sound, when tagged onto the end of a vocalization, translates to something like, "It's coming." So a mother might cheep to her chicks, "Follow me up here! Danger—it's coming!" Or a male strutting in front of a female might tack the cheep to the end of a crow, meaning, "Passion, food, babies, protection—it's coming, girl!" In other words, this cheep works as a rudimentary form of the future tense. This hen, whose brain was lighting up, turning over, working, while she looked up at her hen friends in the cage (hens have long-lasting friendships and can recognize more than a hundred other chicken faces, even after months of separation, and they recognize human faces too), her brain was in the toil of trying to convey the complex thought, *I'll be back for you, I promise*, not a sentence hens would generally have a lot of use for in or out of cages, because they like to stay close to one another, even in the wild. This particular cheep came to her.

She made the sound of her own name—Bwwaauk—and the cheep, "It's coming." Then she slid down the pile of excrement and marched on.

She never did go back.

RALPH BLACK

# Egrets

*In memory of Barry Lopez*

It's good, he said, the way memory
sometimes slips a gauzy film
between the then and the now,

so that the egrets you're sure you saw
flapping over the traffic, just above
the parking structure in the Bronx

where you were walking how many
summer mornings ago, the city's hum
dialing up, the smell of bread from

a bakery, or a bakery truck hacking
spumes of diesel, and three or four
egrets like luffed sails, remaking

incongruity, there they were, and are
still, egrets and not bedsheets tossed
from a high window, three or four, six or

eight egrets and not strewn confetti, not
scraps of notebook paper a city wind
dazzles again into birds, bright flashes

hovering between bird-dream and
reverie of bird, silhouette, intaglio,
origami shadows igniting a city street

and, too, your memory alit and catching,
sometimes, from the corner of an eye
that sudden buffeting flight.

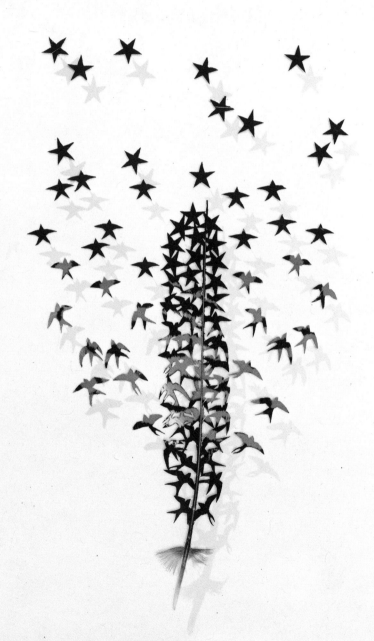

HOW THE STARS WERE MADE

JOHN FREEMAN

# Birds

On the edge of Jardin du Luxembourg nightjars fret
the dark, shrikes pace the grounds, that fierce khanjar
between the eyes. This week chiffchaff clocked in,
flitting branch to branch on stockinged legs, plumage
pale as an emerald soaked in water. Whoever named
them "common" suffers an ordinary mind. Wrens
arrived, too, churring and scolding, singing about love.
Somewhere a peregrine sits above it all in silence,
targeting, eyes ringed in yellow. Valkyrie of dominion.
How often to prey one must be silent and alone.
Whoever named a pistol grip a "bird's head" was
looking at something without wonder, something dead.

Jonathan Trouern-Trend

# Birding Babylon

*Deep in Iraq with a Humvee, a flak jacket, and a passion*

*February 23, 2004*

I N THE SOUTHERN PART of Iraq the landscape is like Kuwait, flat desert with a cast of green from the winter rains. There are a few camels and traditional black Bedouin tents here and there, with large flocks of sheep and goats nearby.

We drove through the southern marshes that were absolutely decimated by Saddam's draining program. He did this to destroy the traditional home of the Marsh Arabs. All along the road were ditches and dug-up ground. For miles and miles the land looked like a giant disorganized construction zone.

The birding is fantastic. I haven't had so many life birds in one day since being in Indonesia in 1990. There are birds everywhere—waterbirds and shorebirds in the pools, land birds flying by or sitting on fences. I can only identify the large and distinctive ones as we whiz by—lots of black-winged stilts, avocets, red-wattled plover, and black-headed gulls. Here's the rest of the list for the day: little grebe, little egret, coot, spur-winged plover, black-tailed godwit, redshank, common sandpiper, slender-billed gull, Armenian gull, rock pigeon, wood pigeon, collared dove, pied kingfisher, crested lark, barn swallow, white (pied) wagtail, white-cheeked bulbul, great gray shrike, isabelline shrike, rook, hooded crow, house sparrow.

*March 16, 2004*

Slowly, I'm getting to know the better birding areas on base. Behind one of the buildings is a great view of a little lagoon surrounded by phragmites. While there I saw a couple of coots, three moorhens chasing each other around in the grass, a magpie flying over the marsh, and a spectacular purple gallinule (not the same species as the one in North America).

Birding on base doesn't usually elicit any undue attention from the MPs. I think that everyone thinks I'm doing security work when I'm looking into the distance with binoculars. I'm not sure what they think when I'm looking up into a tree.

*March 18, 2004*

Crested larks are one of the most common birds in Kuwait and Iraq. They are a bit bigger and plumper than a horned lark and they have a funny little crest on their head that always seems to be sticking straight up. They run a few feet and then stop and look around, repeating this all day long.

On our convoy up from Kuwait, we had to stop because one of the Humvees had a flat. We all piled out of the vehicles and set up a defensive perimeter with our weapons pointing out. It was a bit of a surreal scene, because as I'm lying on the ground with my eye on some guy racing around in a pickup truck, wondering if he's going to take a potshot at us (which would have been suicidal), a pair of crested larks was not even ten feet from me, the male displaying and dancing around.

*April 1, 2004*

Today I had an absolutely fantastic day, finally getting outside the wire into the surrounding farmland while on a civil affairs mission delivering school supplies to children. Keeping my eyes out for new birds, I was trying not to drive the Humvee into an irrigation canal. I did see a few egrets in the fields (maybe cattle egrets) and a group of blue-cheeked bee-eaters hawking for insects and perching on power lines. I wish I had a chance to study the bee-eaters, but I'll probably get to when I go out again.

*April 13, 2004*

We've had a lot of rocket and mortar attacks in the last few days. One day we had eight or nine hit inside the wire. As a result we need to go everywhere in body armor and helmet. So Saturday was a day for birding in full battle rattle—weapon included, of course.

I found a new approach to the junkyard pond, which I drove up to in my Humvee. There was a lot of commotion in the reeds—five or six Dead Sea sparrows darting in and out. They are pretty little birds with a chestnut wing patch and a face marked with black, white, and yellow.

While I was watching the sparrows, a large brown warbler hopped up on one of the reeds. It was my second lifer of the day, a great reed warbler. On the far shore, two spur-winged plovers flew back and forth. Most of the rooks have left and the numbers of black-headed gulls at the dump have dropped dramatically.

*April 25, 2004*

Along one of the side streets near the airstrip I found a pair of Old World warblers hopping around in some large trees. One of them was an icterine warbler. The other was some other nondescript type of *Hippolais* species, possibly an olivaceous warbler.

While I was thumbing through my field guide, a lady came up to me and introduced herself as a fellow birder. She's working here on base as a DoD civilian, I think. She said a white-cheeked bulbul sings outside her window every morning.

At the pond behind the laundry, five white-winged terns were cruising around the reeds. These birds breed in this area, so they might be here to stay. A spectacular white-breasted, or Smyrna, kingfisher perched on the reeds in front of me. It had a big red storklike bill, a reddish brown head, and blue wings, back, and tail.

I think I walked around four or five miles. I had all of my gear on and was completely soaked with sweat when I got back.

*May 3, 2004*

I took the loop road around the perimeter down to the laundry pond, my main birding spot. A couple of the Filipino KBR guys came over and asked what I was looking at. I let them look at the purple swamp hen through my binoculars. They seemed amused that I wanted to look at the birds.

As I walked back along the road, I passed one of the many large cement bunkers here on base. On top of the bunker twenty feet from me was a little owl. It flew away when I got out of my truck, but I came back at dusk and it was sitting in the same place.

*May 6, 2004*

A few days ago, I got to go to the Tigris River to help take water samples. A small, spry bird emerged out of the reeds next to me and hopped around on a log. It was plain-colored with a rufous tail that it held upright like a wren. This new bird for me turned out to be a rufous bush-robin.

*May 13, 2004*

Today we had a sandstorm. The trees were whipping around and clouds of sand were rolling through. I found a broken wood pigeon egg at the base of a tamarisk tree, the wind having thrown it out. The pigeon was still sitting on the nest, so there were probably more. Out back I watched two house sparrows and two white-cheeked bulbuls fruitlessly chasing a large white moth.

I need to get out again soon.

*June 11, 2004*

The summer heat has come. The high temperature is between 105 and 122 degrees during the day. The white-cheeked bulbuls don't seem bothered in the least. They sing, chase each other around, and hop from branch to branch in the tamarisk trees.

Last weekend I had a mission in another location. I was hoping to see some new birds on my trip across the Tigris and out into the desert. Nothing new, but while in the desert, I watched a crested lark hovering a hundred feet off the ground, singing its heart out. The amazing thing is that it kept it up for almost ten minutes, slowly drifting in its hover. Finally it came flying down and rested on the ground near me.

*June 23, 2004*

I got out for four hours on Saturday, 17:30 to 21:30. I started near the north pond, where a couple black-winged stilts came flying out of the reeds. As I was watching some wood pigeons, a pair of F-16s came tearing down the runway with their afterburners going. The noise was incredible as they quickly disappeared into the sky. The birds were unfazed.

*June 30, 2004*

I was talking to one of our local guys and quizzing him on the Arabic names of various birds and animals. He said the white stork is called *lak lak*. They nest on the tops of several mosques in a nearby town. As in the West, the stork is associated with bringing babies. Some of the guys started singing me a local song about the stork, a mother, and a baby.

*August 31, 2004*

We made the trek down to a base near the ruins of ancient Babylon. I stayed right next to the Euphrates River, which is significantly smaller than the Tigris. The camp was dotted with hundreds of date palms, olive and pomegranate trees, and thick reeds next to the river.

The next morning I birded in the ruins of Babylon proper. An Iraq babbler sat obligingly on a fence for a few minutes before diving into the reeds. In the same area I saw a few young white-cheeked bulbuls that were just fledging. A pond near an amphitheater from Alexander the Great's time had a black-crowned night heron, a few little egrets, pied kingfishers, and black-winged stilts.

Near the ruins I saw my first laughing dove. It was walking around near the base of a date tree. I really enjoyed the combination of the lush surroundings, the birds, and the history of Babylon, not to mention that this base is much safer than mine—it almost never gets attacked.

I returned to Baghdad and took another walk to the scrubby area near the lake. I was treated to a great view of an immature isabelline shrike hunting insects along a dirt berm. I also saw two male black francolins—large chicken-size game birds—chasing each other around in the scrub. When I got too close to them, they flew a short distance on their broad, short wings and scurried away into the brush. The birds were spectacular, with their black bellies, deep chestnut collars, and white cheek patches.

*September 14, 2004*

Recently I've had some fantastic views of hoopoe, certainly one of the most distinctive birds I've seen in the area. When they fly, they almost look like a broad-winged woodpecker, with their striking black-and-white wings. Their body is a buff color and they have a crest that they can move up and down. One day, one landed next to the edge of the pond, about fifty feet from me. I spent ten minutes watching it hop around in the mud, catching insects, and every so often stopping, cocking its head to one side, and erecting its crest in full glory. Some of the local people believe that the hoopoe, or *hudhud* in Arabic, has magical powers. Its bones are used in potions and magical charms.

*October 24, 2004*

Waiting at the starting line for the Army ten-miler race to begin, I looked up and saw a flock of six rooks slowly flying over—the first ones I've seen since spring.

*October 28, 2004*

The rooks have officially arrived in numbers. These very social crows will be spending the winter. At dawn for the past two mornings, great scraggly flocks of rooks mixed with a few jackdaws poured over our base, moving from their roosts to the freshly plowed fields. Around noon I saw a huge kettle of several hundred rooks circling upward in a thermal. For a few minutes it was a perfect cylinder of circling black birds fifty feet wide and a couple hundred feet high. A rook tornado.

*November 5, 2004*

A few days ago, I traveled to a forward operating base near Mosul. As we helicoptered north above the lush green agricultural lands bordering the Tigris, I watched hundreds of egrets and small flocks of rooks and hooded crows. Our low-altitude flight flushed a large flock of sociable plovers.

A houbara bustard flew up from the dry scrub, showing large white patches on its wings. These game birds are sometimes hunted by trained falcons in Arab countries. Its current breeding status in Iraq is unknown, according to my field guide, which just has a big question mark on the distribution map.

*November 10, 2004*

The rooks are much more playful than the crows and jackdaws, and much more acrobatic. One sat in our big eucalyptus tree and made a racket while we were trying to hold a formation.

One night this week, I drove around our perimeter. I saw lots of little rodents running around, a little owl flying across the road, and a golden jackal. The jackals and foxes are constantly tunneling under our fence, tormenting the security patrol, which doesn't appreciate any holes.

*November 14, 2004*

I made a quick trip down to the International (Green) Zone yesterday. Our helicopter dodged birds all the way to Baghdad. Big flocks of wood pigeons and collared doves flew up from the trees into our path. In the flooded fields below there were some cattle egrets and small shorebirds.

Driving around the base today, I found that hundreds of gulls had returned to our burn pit/dump. I didn't have a chance to see what species they were but I'll have plenty of chances—they'll be here all winter.

OWL HUNT

KURT BROWN

# Lines While the War Widens

We kept a calm proprietary watch,
my wife and I, over a clutch of robins
in a filthy nest gathered
of dry wattles wedged under the eaves
of our ranch-house roof.

Small as she was, the careful mother caught
my eye darting past my window
where I worked thralled in a stupor
of vague words that crawled
left to right, woven together in a warp of sense,

home for any meaning that might hatch there,
frail and hopeful
as those skinny necks that shot up
whenever she arrived
to stuff their bellies with a delicate bug.

Those little beaks would snap apart
to gobble worms plucked
from steaming earth, unseemly strips
of raw flesh, flecked with dirt
that passed for food among the feathered.

How can I make romance out of nature
when their mother crammed
their guts with such revolting stuff
then stooped behind to ferry
off the chalky pellets of their own scat?

Or when the magpie, black and hooded
like a killer, swooped to stab
the first chick lucky enough to leave
that nest, took its head clean
off with a deft stroke of his polished bill?

And when I chased the killer, lean
and sullen, only half afraid
of this galumphing hero full of feckless noise,
he seemed but scant impressed,
half inclined to circle back and claim his prize.

Headless body on a green ground,
mindless as dumb nature:
death was your mother, spring your first
birthday and tomb. Welcome
here, little brother. Welcome home.

TERRY TEMPEST WILLIAMS

# Gods Among Us

*Erosion and the resurrection of belief*

ONUMENT VALLEY is a hallucination without drugs. It is
a kaleidoscope of colors that turns by the sun's wrist. Red
sandstone bleeds into pink and deepens into lavender, fad-
ing into blue until sunset offers a surprise encore of golden
light, and we watch the desert glow. We spent the night here after a full day
of storytelling shared inside the Diné Welcome Center. We were in Indian
Country. From dawn until dusk, stories wrapped around us like Pendleton
blankets. Everyone was invited—Hopi, Tewa, Ute Mountain Ute, and Diné
(or Navajo), Native and non-Native people alike. Time expanded; what we
imagined in the telling became truth.

I WAS WITH Fazal Sheikh, an American photographer who lives in Switzer-
land. We were guests of Utah Diné Bikéyah, a nonprofit organization committed to protecting Bears Ears National Monument.

We had been traveling together in a spirit of collaboration, experimenting
with image and text, visiting friends along the way. After President Trump's
evisceration of Bears Ears and Grand Staircase–Escalante National Monuments, these desert lands seemed much more vulnerable.

The spring winds had come, and with them, dust devils that whipped
up the sands like banshees. It's a volatile time in the red rock desert. The
Bureau of Land Management (BLM) had just held an online oil and gas lease
sale in Utah, successfully securing bids from fossil fuel companies for 45
parcels of lands, 51,400 acres, the majority of them in southeastern Utah.
Many of them are near the ancestral Puebloan villages of Hovenweep, home

to 2,500 people between AD 1200 and 1300 who left a rich and distinctive record of habitation, from towers built on boulders to intricate mosaiclike stone-constructed dwellings and ceremonial kivas.

The United States government is continuing the destabilization of other national monuments with its insatiable appetite for fossil fuel development, as if gutting Bears Ears and Grand Staircase–Escalante National Monuments was not enough. Add Hovenweep National Monument and Canyons of the Ancients National Monument to the Department of the Interior's list of desecration sites, yet another violent assault on Native people and ancestral burial grounds.

The National Park Service asked the BLM to hold off thirteen of their leases in close proximity to these archaeologically rich monuments. The BLM refused.

WHAT DOES it mean to refuse?

REFUSE rə'fyo͞oz (verb)
1. indicate or show that one is not willing to do something. "I refused to answer."
2. indicate that one is not willing to accept or grant (something offered or requested). "She refused a cigarette."

And what are other ways to refuse?

| | | |
|---|---|---|
| • decline | • dodge | • hold out |
| • ignore | • evade | • make excuses |
| • protest | • nix | • not budge |
| • rebuff | • regret | • not budget |
| • reject | • repel | • not buy |
| • turn down | • reprobate | • not care to |
| • withdraw | • repudiate | • pass up |
| • withhold | • shun | • refuse to receive |
| • demur | • spurn | • send off |
| • desist | • beg off | • set aside |
| • disaccord | • brush off | • turn away |
| • disallow | • dispense with | • turn a deaf ear to |
| • disapprove | • hold back | • turn from |
| • dissent | • hold off | • turn one's back on |

It is the last synonym that feels the most accurate to me: *to turn one's back on.*

Donald Trump's Bureau of Land Management is turning its back on beauty.

My belief in the federal government's ability to steward an American ethic of place is eroding. We must decouple environmental protection and the health of our public lands and the communities adjacent to them from both the political Right and Left. Neither side is to be trusted. And those we can trust may not be able to go far enough.

We must look to each other to find enduring ways to honor, respect, and protect the life that surrounds us.

I refuse to comply with the rules and ruthlessness of this administration's actions. I believe, as Abbey said, "We will outlive the bastards."

BELIEF IS TRICKY. One day I do. One day I don't. There are things I believe that have never wavered, but my belief in God is not one of those.

Not long ago, I made a list, my attempt to address the question: "Do I believe in God?" It went like this:

God as an old white man with a beard —*No.*
God as a human—*No.*
God as a being —*No.*
God as energy—*Yes.*
God as consequential—*Don't know.*
God without definition—*Yes.*
God as a creative force in the Universe—*Yes.*
God as natural processes in motion—*Yes.*
God as evolution—*Yes.*
God as gravity—*Yes.*
God as love—*Yes.*
God as forgiveness—*Yes.*
God as beauty—*Yes.*
God as a no and a yes—*Maybe.*
God as wrathful and merciful—*Perhaps. This one scares me.*
God as Mystery—*Most certainly.*

I realized through my exercise that my problem is with the word *God*, for all
the limitations it has placed on my imagination, such as "God the Father."
Looking back, this was the beginning of my erosion with Mormonism in
particular and religion in general. It happened early. I watched and studied
birds. If I dreamed of a great horned owl and saw one the next day, that
was normal, to be expected. If a yellow warbler came into my mind, it was
not unusual for me to hear one. As a child, I came to understand that my
relationship with nature was reciprocal and that nature had a relationship
with me. We called to one another. We called one another into being. What I
mean by that is we have evolved together. I still have a tailbone. I trust what
I see, and I believe what I feel. Trusting direct experience is the open door to
revelation. This was my foundation for faith. It still is.

WE HAD BEEN brought into a waking dream where hundreds of people
gathered in the desert somewhere between Utah and Arizona. (State lines
mean little in Indian Country.) We climbed up a hill with our vehicle and
abruptly dropped down into a sizable clearing of sage where dozens of pick-
ups were parked. We parked next to them and walked to where eight bonfires
burned, four on each side of an open space reserved for what was to come.
Families and friends gathered around the fires in silence. Some stood. Some
sat on folding chairs. Waiting. Watching. We were the guests of Jonah Yel-
lowman, a medicine person and the spiritual advisor for Utah Diné Bikéyah.
Tonight was the last of the Yeibichai dances. Jonah had spoken of the Blue
Bird People. Our host gave us this explanation in his pickup truck before we
entered the community in firelight: ceremony moves us from sadness to joy,
from feeling numb to feeling alive, to being part of a community instead of
being isolated, as one often feels on long winter nights in the red rock amphitheater of wildness. We drove the rest of the washboard road with the constel-
lations as our maps. Orion was rising above the southern horizon.

We were touching the outer circumference of something that was not
ours, but something we could feel in our shared desire for balance and
renewal on the eve of the spring equinox. What is the reach of ceremony?

Piñon smoke rose from two structures where the dancers would begin
and where they would end. The smell of burning cedar permeated the
grounds. And then, the sound of rattles began. Before our eyes, faces the
color of midnight blue became birds became dancers whose high-pitched

voices called forth the spring as winter surrendered. The repetitive chants wrapped us into a trance, and I forgot the cold and closed my eyes, remembering the sweet songs of bluebirds that greet us each April. Those in need of healing were met by the winged ones, who restored their spirits by calling out the wounds of grief and discord housed as disease in the body. We watched sparks from the fires rise as exclamation points.

It was just as we had been told, but could not have imagined. The Blue Bird People arrived through a haze of wafting smoke, dancing and singing through the corridors of fire, realigning the world with each deliberate gesture. Hands raised, rattles held, shimmering apparitions born of the stars. These night dwellers have a name that will not be named. Those who called for a healing will remain unknown. Those who stood in the ripples of their power were stirred. We were folded into the tightly woven cloth of community, even as guests.

WE LEFT THE GATHERING in the wee hours of the morning, and Jonah drove us back to where we were staying. He got out of his truck and walked us to our rooms. With the Pleiades above us, he turned to me and said, "Now, you have a story to tell."

"But this is not mine to tell," I said.

"You will find it—the story that is yours."

BACK HOME in Castle Valley, Fazal and I got out of the car. Two bluebirds, male and female, were flying over our house. They landed in the cottonwood not yet clothed in leaves. Brooke met us at the front door and noted they were the first bluebirds he had seen this year.

We set the table and cooked dinner. We talked. We slept. We dreamed.

When I awoke in the morning, I saw the shadows of birds, wings hovering outside, silhouettes appearing inside on the blinds. Bluebirds. Through the wooden slats, I watched a female bluebird treading air with her wings, her blue-feathered body suspended. She was staring in my direction, with her small black eyes and black beak slightly opened. I believed she was seeing her own reflection in the window.

Another bluebird, turquoise in sunlight, came up behind her. She rose, he rose, in a fluttering of wings, and then both disappeared into a circular opening in the overhang of the roof that once housed a light—a perfect place for a nest. The courting birds flew out, each in a different direction. The female returned to the window—hovering—and our gaze met once again. I held my breath so I wouldn't scare her as she flew in place, our eyes never leaving each other. I left the window and moved to the window seat, where she followed me—still hovering—still focused. It was as though she wanted to come inside. He, too, followed her and pulled his turquoise wings forward and backward with an intensity that bordered on urgency or panic or both.

Brooke was my witness. Together, we opened all the doors in the house, and then he left for the day.

Fazal rose, and we prepared breakfast. The table was reset. The coffee was made and poured. Scrambled eggs, mixed with onions and green chilies, were steaming on the plate. We were about to sit down together. Instead, as if called by something unheard, I walked out of the kitchen to the far window in the bedroom, where I had last seen the bluebirds' flurry of wings. In the corner, the male bluebird sat between the blinds and the window. To my astonishment, he was not anxious, but calm. I slowly raised the blinds and knelt beside him. He let me slide my right hand beneath his breast and cup my left hand around his back. I felt his beating heart through his feathered chest. I stood up with the bluebird in hand, and as I walked into the living room, he cocked his head and I saw my own reflection in his small black eyes. I quietly called to Fazal. He met me in the living room, smiled, and gently stroked the bluebird's head. We carried him outside, where a flock of bluebirds were flying near the house. I opened my hands; the bluebird flew, joining the others, and then, disappeared.

Just like that.

CAN WE ever know the reach of ceremony?

MY BROTHER HANK works with his hands day in and day out, digging trenches, laying pipe that natural gas or water or sewage might flow through. At night he makes art, creating sculptures from the cut and remaindered steel pipe he puts in the ground. He also uses the discarded detritus of machinery he finds to make his pieces. I cannot name the parts, but when Hank welds them together, he creates objects of wholeness and beauty: a dancer in an arabesque of twisted metal, a woman in prayer, lovers entwined.

For Christmas, Hank made me a Bird Man—his arms outstretched like wings, now rusted and mottled. His eyes look straight ahead. The beak is pronounced. The Bird Man's right knee is bent; his left foot is about to be raised in dance. I did not see the full measure of my brother's creation, nor how prescient the Bird Man would be, until now as the flock of bluebirds encircled him.

My BELIEF in nature is the nature of my faith as a human being humbled before the gods we live among. The god made in my own image that I was introduced to as a child now circles the fire with all the other gods—those with feathers, fins, and fur, scales and tails and multiple legs that crawl among the flowers, plants, and trees. Stories can be understood in a myriad of languages. Translation becomes a matter of listening to what one feels as well as to what one hears. I do not view this communion with other species as an act of idolatry or witchcraft or momentary madness, but rather the practice of good manners among neighbors, where peace is maintained through mutual respect and consideration. We learn from one another. Without manners, violence enters the room. Without the decency of imagination, narcissism leads.

For many of us raised in Christian traditions, a personalization of God in human form is eroding. Human exceptionalism is destroying the living world. For me, a providential faith rooted in religion has evolved into a cosmic faith that supports a conscious unity within all Creation. When I held the bluebird in my hands, I was also holding my own liberation. This is not a metaphor but "an ecology of mind," where we can change the nature of reality through our focused attention, which is another form of prayer.

Earth has always been a sphere of geologic forces capable of rupturing the surface of things, but now we too are force fields of consciousness capable of shifting fixed patterns of thinking. This is the enlightened Anthropocene, not just the destructive one.

If we are to flourish as a species, an erosion of belief will be necessary, one that says we are not the center of the universe but a dynamic part of an expanding and contracting future that celebrates and collaborates with uncertainty. The perpetuation of biblical self-identification is harming us and everything else on this planet we call home. Recognizing the dignity of each living thing, mobile or fixed, insect, animal, tree, or mushroom, has broadened my love for this world and diminished my need for a god in heaven. We have multitudes of gods on Earth. ·

What is ceremony but a reminder of the power we can summon together? A sense of harmony is remembered and comes to us in the way of dreams that present themselves outside the normal parameters of time and space. It is also sacred teachings passed on through time. A guide appears with an invitation to participate in something mysterious where we yield to that which cannot be named. We can say yes or no, but sooner or later we can no longer deny that if we continue to stand on the front lines of pain without a deeper understanding of what we intend for our children and those who follow them, we are a species devoted to death. The future is created through actions—good and evil. We are called to serve the beauty that hovers just beyond our reach, outside, because we intuit what we lack inside—enthusiasm—which comes from the Greek word *entheos*, meaning "the god within." Our task is to open the doors for this reunion.

BUSHTIT NESTS

Benjamin Gucciardi

# The Nest

*For Alfredo Espino*

This morning
I watched a goldfinch
Disappear into a tree
Through a hole no bigger

Than my open mouth.
From the hollow
The bird
Began her crooning.

That's what poetry is
I thought—
Not the tree,
But the hidden song.

Not the yellow bird,
But the instinct to climb
Inside the darkness
To sing.

ELIZABETH KOLBERT

# Eclipse

ONE EVENING in January 1834, a young minister named James Freeman Clarke was sitting in his parlor in Louisville, Kentucky, when a boy came to the door with a strange note. It was from the celebrated Shakespearean actor Junius Brutus Booth (father of John Wilkes), who was playing at a local theater.

Booth, the note said, was "looking for a place of interment for his friend," or perhaps it was "friends"; there was an odd mark at the end of the word. Clarke hurried over to the actor's hotel, eager to console him, but Booth seemed disinclined to talk about his loss.

Was the death very sudden? the minister inquired.

"Very," Booth replied.

Was he a relative?

"Distant," Booth said.

The conversation wandered. Booth recited Coleridge's "The Rime of the Ancient Mariner" and Lord Byron's "Epitaph to a Dog." Finally he asked if Clarke would "like to look at the remains." He led the minister into an adjoining room, where, spread out on a sheet, were the bodies of a dozen birds. They were elegant creatures, with slender necks and tapering tail feathers. Some were all brown; others shimmered in blue and green. They were passenger pigeons. Booth took up one of the birds and held it to his heart.

"You see these innocent victims of man's barbarity?" he said. "I wish to testify, in some public way, against this wanton destruction of life. And I wish you to help me. Will you?"

A HUNDRED and eighty years later, Booth's question still hangs in the
air, which is why I am standing in a gallery at the Massachusetts Museum
of Contemporary Art, trying to talk to a pair of artists over the drone of a
power drill.

The artists, Edward Morris and Susannah Sayler, are setting up a video
installation that might be thought of as a memorial to a lost experience. Its
aim is to reproduce the marvel of watching a flock of passenger pigeons,
hundreds of millions of birds strong, sweep across the sky.

Many accounts have come down to us of what this was like. When a flock
passed overhead, these reports suggest, it was both scary and astonishing,
menacing and mesmerizing. John James Audubon, who encountered a
flock in western Kentucky in 1813, described the air as "literally filled with
pigeons." The "light of noonday," he wrote, "was obscured as by an eclipse."

Morris and Sayler are working in a long gallery with a fifty-foot-high
ceiling. The windows have been blacked out, and on the back wall, they've
projected an enormous tree, only in negative, so that its limbs are white. The
birds, also white, arrive from the west and descend on the tree in a frenzy of
flapping wings. Then they take off again, first in small numbers, later in a
great mass. They stream across the ceiling, but instead of darkening the sky,
as the real birds once did, the bird images light it up. The absent are made
present, in a ghostly form.

Back in Booth's day, actual flocks of passenger pigeons would block the
sun for days at a time. In Morris and Sayler's version, the flight takes just
seven minutes, and features 266,982 individual birds. Sayler explains to
me that just as there are no living passenger pigeons left, there are also no
computer-generated ones, so they've had to rely on a program that anima-
tors developed to simulate the flight of ordinary rock pigeons. The species
are only distantly related; passengers were longer and thinner, with more
tapered wings. Morris and Sayler have had the program tweaked to better
match the extinct birds' shape.

At this late stage (in 2014)—the very last passenger pigeon, a bird named
Martha, died more than a hundred years ago—it's impossible to say how
close the projection comes to re-creating the original experience. Audubon's 1813 account includes a vivid description of pigeon dung falling from
the sky like "melting flakes of snow." But when the windows have all been
blocked and the drilling stops, the experience of watching the ghostly flock

is unquestionably powerful. It is also disorienting in a way that, it occurs to me, Booth would have welcomed.

Though sympathetic to Booth, Clarke ultimately refused to help him "testify" against the wanton destruction. A few days after their meeting, Clarke learned that Booth had proceeded without him. The actor had purchased a cemetery plot, had a coffin made, and had arranged for a funeral service to be recited for the dead pigeons. For several days, according to Clarke, Booth "continued to visit the grave of his little friends, and mourned over them with a grief which did not seem at all theatrical."

GOODBYE

MARY OLIVER

# Morning Light

Every morning
   the good news
      pours
         through the field

touching
   every blossom,
      every stem,
         and each of them,

on the instant,
   offers to be part of it—
      offers to lift and hold, willingly,
         the vast burden of light

all day.
   In my life
      I have never seen it to fail—
         flower after flower,

leaf after pearly leaf,
   to the acre,
      to the massy many,
         is silvered, is flooded;

and such voices
    spangle among it—
        larks and sparrows—
            all those small souls—

are everywhere
    tossing the quick wheels of pleasure
        from their red throats
            as they hang on—

as though on little masts
    of golden ships,
        to the tops of the weeds—
            and that's when I come—

that's when I come, crying out to the world:
    oh give me a corner of it
        to lift also, to sing about, to touch
            with my wild hands—and they do.

BRIAN DOYLE

# Raptorous

I HAVE BEEN so hawk-addled and owl-absorbed and falcon-haunted and eagle-maniacal since I was a little kid that it was a huge shock to me to discover that there were people who did *not* think that seeing a sparrow hawk helicoptering over an empty lot and then dropping like an anvil and o my god *coming up with wriggling lunch* was the coolest thing ever.

I mean, who could possibly not be awed by a tribe whose various members can see a rabbit clearly from a mile away (eagles), fly sideways through tree branches like feathered fighter jets (wood hawks), look like tiny brightly colored linebackers (kestrels, with their cool gray helmets), hunt absolutely silently on the wing (owls), fly faster than any other being on Earth (falcons), and can spot a trout from fifty feet in the air, gauge piscine speed and direction, and nail the dive and light-refraction and wind-gust and trout-startle so perfectly that it snags three fish a day (our friend the osprey)? Not to mention they *look* cool—they are seriously large, they have muscles on their muscles, they are stone-cold efficient hunters with built-in butchery tools, and all of them have this stern *I could kick your ass but I am busy* look, which took me years to discover was not a general simmer of surliness but a result of the supraorbital ridge protecting their eyes.

And they are more *adamant* than other birds. They arrest your attention. You see a hawk, and you stop what minor crime you are committing and pay close attention to a craft master who commands the horizon until he or she is done and drifts airily away, terrifying the underbrush. You see an eagle, you gape; you hear the piercing whistle of an osprey along the river, you stand motionless and listen with reverence; you see an owl launch at dusk, like a burly gray dream against the last light, you flinch a little, and are awed, and count yourself blessed.

They inspire fear, too—that should be said. They carry switchblades and know how to use them, they back down from no one, and there are endless stories of eagles carrying away babies and kittens and cubs left unattended for a fateful moment in meadows and clearings, and falcons shearing off the eyebrows of idiots climbing to their nests, and owls casually biting off the fingers of people who discover Fluffy is actually Ferocious. A friend of mine deep in the Oregon forest, for example, tells the story of watching a gyrfalcon descend upon his chickens and grab one with a daggered fist as big as my friend's fist, but with much better weaponry, and then rise again easily into the fraught and holy air while, reports my friend with grudging admiration, the bird glared at him with the clear and inarguable message, *I am taking this chicken, and you are not going to be a fool and mess with me.*

I suppose what I am talking about here really is awe and reverence and some kind of deep thrumming respect for beings who are very good at what they do and fit into this world with remarkable sinewy grace. We are all hunters in the end, bruised and battered and broken in various ways, and we seek always to rise again, and fit deftly into the world, and soar to our uppermost reaches, enduring with as much grace as we can. Maybe the reason that so many human beings are as hawk-addled and owl-absorbed and falcon-haunted and eagle-maniacal as me is because we wish to live like them, to use them like stars to steer by, to remember to be as alert and unafraid as they are. Maybe being raptorous is in some way rapturous. Maybe what the word *rapture* really means is an attention so ferocious that you see the miracle of the world as the miracle it is. Maybe that is what happens to saints and mystics who float up into the air and soar beyond sight and vanish finally into the glare of the sun.

CROW WANDER

# BIOGRAPHIES

RALPH BLACK is the author of the poetry collections *Bloom and Laceration* and *Turning Over the Earth*. He teaches at SUNY Brockport.

KURT BROWN (1944–2013) founded the Aspen Writers' Conference and Writers' Conferences and Centers. He was the author of more than a dozen chapbooks and full-length collections of poetry, and editor of another ten poetry anthologies. He taught for many years at Sarah Lawrence College in New York.

ROBERT CORDING taught English and creative writing at College of the Holy Cross for thirty-eight years and then worked as a poetry mentor in the Seattle Pacific University MFA program. He has published nine collections of poems, the latest of which is *In the Unwalled City*.

TOM CRAWFORD is the author of six previous books of poetry, most recently *The Names of Birds*. This poem was later collected in *The Names of Birds*, copyright © 2011. Reprinted by permission of Sherman Asher Publishing.

ALISON HAWTHORNE DEMING's most recent books include *A Woven World: On Fashion, Fishermen, and the Sardine Dress* and *Zoologies: On Animals and the Human Spirit*. The recipient of a Guggenheim Fellowship, Stegner Fellowship at Stanford University, National Endowment for the Arts fellowships, and Walt Whitman Award, she is Regents Professor at the University of Arizona. This poem was later included in *Science and Other Poems* by Alison Hawthorne Deming, copyright © 1994. Reprinted by permission of Louisiana State University Press.

BRIAN DOYLE (1956–2017) was the editor of *Portland* magazine and a long-time contributor to *Orion*, as well as the *New York Times*, *The Atlantic*, and *Harper's*. In 2008 he received the American Academy of Arts and Letters Award in Literature.

BLAS FALCONER is the author of three poetry collections, most recently *Forgive the Body This Failure*. He is the poetry editor for *The Los Angeles Review* and teaches in the low-residency MFA at Murray State University.

JONATHAN FRANZEN is a novelist, essayist, journalist, translator, screenwriter, and bird-watcher. His most recent books are the novel *Crossroads* and the essay collection *The End of the End of the Earth*. A longtime board member of the American Bird Conservancy, Franzen has received the Euro-Natur Award and the Utah Award in the Environmental Humanities for his advocacy on behalf of birds.

JOHN FREEMAN is the author of several books of poetry and prose, including *Dictionary of the Undoing* and *Wind, Trees*, and the editor of *The Penguin Book of the Modern American Short Story* and, with Tracy K. Smith, *There's a Revolution Outside, My Love*. The founder of the literary annual *Freeman's*, he is an executive editor at Alfred A. Knopf. This poem was later collected in *The Park* by John Freeman, copyright © 2020. Reprinted here by permission of Copper Canyon Press.

DAVID GESSNER is the author of ten books, including the *New York Times* bestseller *All the Wild That Remains*. He has taught environmental writing as a Briggs-Copeland Lecturer at Harvard and is currently a professor at the University of North Carolina at Wilmington, where he founded the award-winning literary journal *Ecotone*.

MARIANA GOSNELL (1932–2012) was a medicine reporter for *Newsweek* and a regular contributor to *Smithsonian*. She was the author of *Zero Three Bravo: Solo Across America in a Small Plane* and *Ice: The Nature, the History, and the Uses of an Astonishing Substance*.

BENJAMIN GUCCIARDI is the author of the poetry collection *West Portal* and the chapbook *I Ask My Sister's Ghost*. He works with refugee and immigrant youth in Oakland, California, through Soccer Without Borders, an organization he founded in 2006.

KIMIKO HAHN is the author of ten collections of poems. Her honors include a Guggenheim Fellowship, a PEN/Voelcker Award, and a Theodore Roethke Memorial Poetry Prize. She is a distinguished professor at Queens College, CUNY.

JIM HARRISON (1937–2016) was the author of more than three dozen books, including *Legends of the Fall* and *Dalva*, and served as the food columnist for the magazines *Brick* and *Esquire*. He published fourteen volumes of poetry. His work has been translated into two dozen languages and produced as four feature-length films. In 2007, he was elected into the American Academy of Arts and Letters. This poem was later collected in the *Complete Poems* by the James T. Harrison Trust, copyright © 2021. Reprinted here by permission of Copper Canyon Press.

SEAN HILL is the author of *Dangerous Goods*, winner of the Minnesota Book Award. He has received fellowships and grants from Cave Canem, the Bush Foundation, the MacDowell Colony, the University of Wisconsin, Bread Loaf Writers' Conference, The Jerome Foundation, and Stanford University, where he was a Wallace Stegner Fellow in Poetry.

KATHLEEN JAMIE is a poet and essayist whose books include *The Tree House*, *The Overhaul*, and *The Bonniest Companie*, which won the Saltire Society Scottish Poetry Book of the Year Award. Her essay in this book was later collected in *Sightlines* by Kathleen Jamie, copyright © 2012. Reprinted by permission of The Experiment press.

W. TODD KANEKO is the author of the poetry books *This Is How the Bone Sings* and *The Dead Wrestler Elegies*, and coauthor of *Poetry: A Writer's Guide and Anthology*. A Kundiman Fellow, he teaches creative writing at Grand Valley State University.

ELIZABETH KOLBERT is the author of several books on climate and science, including *The Sixth Extinction*, for which she won the Pulitzer Prize. For her work at *The New Yorker*, where she's a staff writer, she has received two

National Magazine Awards and the Blake-Dodd Prize from the American Academy of Arts and Letters.

J. DREW LANHAM is the author of *The Home Place: Memoirs of a Colored Man's Love Affair with Nature*. He is a birder, naturalist, hunter-conservationist, MacArthur Award recipient, and Alumni Distinguished Professor of Wildlife Ecology and Master Teacher at Clemson University.

LI-YOUNG LEE's poetry has earned numerous honors, including a Lannan Literary Award, a Paterson Poetry Prize, and an American Book Award. This poem was later collected in *Behind My Eyes* by Li-Young Lee, copyright © 2008. Used by permission of W. W. Norton & Company, Inc.

FRED MARCHANT is the author of five poetry collections, most recently *Said Not Said*. He is the editor of *Another World Instead: The Early Poems of William Stafford*.

CLEOPATRA MATHIS has published eight books of poems, most recently *After the Body*. In 1982, she founded the creative writing program at Dartmouth College. This poem was later collected in *Book of Dogs* by Cleopatra Mathis, copyright © 2012. Reprinted by permission of Sarabande Books.

CHRIS MAYNARD, a Pacific Northwest author, naturalist, and artist, carves feathers into shadow boxes and installations using tiny tools and a family heirloom magnifying glass. While feathers are often perceived as delicate, they are actually quite tough, having to keep a bird clothed, sheltered, and in flight. Maynard's intricate art is included in collections and publications in North America, Asia, Europe, and Australia and featured in his book, *Feathers, Form & Function*.

JEAN MONAHAN is the author of three books of poetry, including *Hands*, which was chosen by Donald Hall for the Anhinga Prize. This poem was later included in *Mauled Illusionist* by Jean Monahan, copyright © 2006. Reprinted here by permission of Orchises Press.

Emily Raboteau is author of *The Professor's Daughter* and *Searching for Zion*, for which she received the American Book Award. She is the Stuart Z. Katz Professor in the Humanities and the Arts at City College of New York.

William Stafford (1914–1993) published more than sixty books comprising four thousand poems. He won the National Book Award in 1963 and served as the poetry consultant to the Library of Congress.

Sandra Steingraber is the author of *Living Downstream* and several other books about climate change, ecology, and the links between human health and the environment. She was an *Orion* columnist for six years.

Jonathan Trouern-Trend was a member of the 118th Area Support Medical Battalion of the Connecticut National Guard. He is the author of *Birding Babylon: A Soldier's Journal from Iraq.*

Deb Olin Unferth is a novelist and essayist whose books include *Barn 8* and *Revolution: The Year I Fell in Love and Went to Join the War.* An associate professor at the University of Texas at Austin, she is also the director of the Pen-City Writers, a creative writing program at a South Texas penitentiary. This story was later included in *Barn 8* by Deb Olin Unferth, copyright © 2020. Reprinted by permission of Graywolf Press.

Terry Tempest Williams is the author of *When Women Were Birds, Erosion,* and *Refuge: An Unnatural History of Family and Place,* among other books. She is the writer in residence at Harvard Divinity School. "Gods Among Us" appeared in *Erosion* (as "Bluebirds") by Terry Tempest Williams. Copyright © 2019 by Terry Tempest Williams. Reprinted by permission of Sarah Crichton Books, an imprint of Farrar, Straus and Giroux. All rights reserved.

## ABOUT *ORION* MAGAZINE

*Orion* is a nonprofit, ad-free, quarterly magazine whose mission is to invite readers into a community of caring for the planet. Since its first issue was published in 1982, *Orion* has sought to explore and enrich the mysterious connections between people and the environments we inhabit, inspiring new thinking about how humanity might live on Earth justly, sustainably, and joyously.

*Contributing Editors*
Kerri Arsenault, John Freeman, Ross Gay, Lacy Johnson, J. Drew Lanham, Sy Montgomery, Emily Raboteau, Elizabeth Rush, Meera Subramanian

*Advisors*
Jad Abumrad, Manish Bapna, Wendell Berry, Eula Biss, David James Duncan, Jane Goodall, Jane Hirshfield, Linda Hogan, Elizabeth Kolbert, Bill McKibben, Lulu Miller, Michael Pietsch, Michael Pollan, Maria Popova, Mary Roach, Scott Russell Sanders, Paul Slovak, Gary Snyder, Rebecca Solnit, Rob Spillman, Sandra Steingraber, Krista Tippett, Mary Evelyn Tucker

Print or digital subscriptions can be purchased at orionmagazine.org, where you can also find posters, tote bags, and other merchandise. Visit orionmagazine.org/workshops for more information about virtual and in-person opportunities to share your work with award-winning authors.

The work featured in this volume was made possible by generous donations from readers and foundations. To learn how you can support *Orion*, visit orionmagazine.org/waystogive, call (888) 909-6568 ext. 14, or e-mail development@orionmagazine.org.

SHORT-STEM GRASS SPARROWS

More books from *Orion* magazine

*To Eat with Grace*
*Animals & People*
*Leave No Child Inside*
*Wonder and Other Survival Skills*
*Change Everything Now*
*Thirty-Year Plan*
*Beyond Ecophobia*
*Place-Based Education*
*Earthly Love*
*The Most Radical Thing You Can Do*
*Old Growth*
*The Book of Bugs*